W9-BCU-438

DINGO

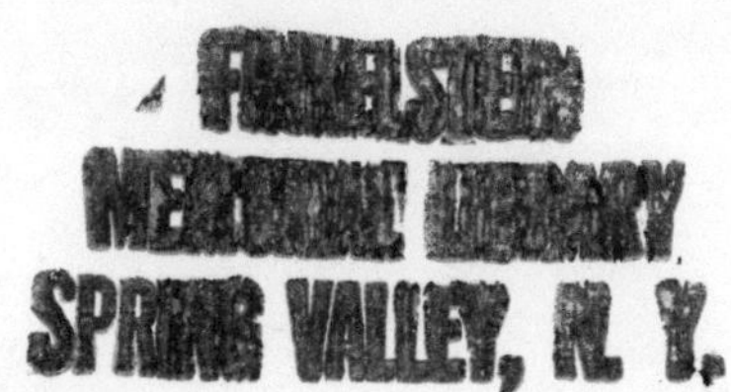

DINGO

A Play By

CHARLES WOOD

822.914
Woo

GROVE PRESS, INC., NEW YORK

70-06337

Copyright © 1967 By Charles Wood

All Rights Reserved

Library of Congress Catalog Card

Number: 79–84885

First Evergreen Edition, 1969

First Printing

CAUTION: This play is fully protected, in whole, in part, or in any form under the copyright laws of the United States of America, the British Empire including the Dominion of Canada, and all other countries of the Copyright Union, and is subject to royalty. All rights, including professional, amateur, motion picture, radio, television, recitation, public reading, and any method of photographic reproduction, are strictly reserved. For professional and amateur rights all inquiries should be addressed to Margaret Ramsay Ltd., 14a Goodwin's Court, London W.C.2, England.

MANUFACTURED IN THE UNITED STATES OF AMERICA

Dingo was first performed in this version at the Bristol Arts Centre on April 28, 1967. Directed by Geoffrey Reeves and designed by Charles Wood, it had the following cast:

DINGO	Tom Kempinski
MOGG	Leon Lissek
TANKY	Mark Jones
NAVIGATING OFFICER	Esmond Rideout
COMIC	Henry Woolf
HERO COLONEL/FIRST BLONDE	Eric Allan
HERO DIGGER/SECOND BLONDE	David Taylor
HERO SCOT/THIRD BLONDE	Colin Fisher
HERO SIKH/FOURTH BLONDE	Alan Moore
HERO POM/FIFTH BLONDE	Ian Lavender
HERO BRUMMIE/WILLIE	Neil Cunningham
DOT AND CARRY ONE	Royston Brimble

Act One

Set in the whole of the Western Desert during the second world war against the Germans—all of it—from a small bit of it.

Clean war.

MOGG *and* DINGO *are dressed in khaki gone yellow trousers/shorts with webbing equipment battle order faded almost white, and boots scuffed white, hair bleached white.*

Legs where you can see them through tatters and between short skirt of MOGG'S *shorts and his hose tops/puttees are deep black brown red splashed with gentian violet.*

Faces are burned bloated splashed with gentian violet. Arms likewise.

MOGG: You've got a bloated face and your limbs are bloated up.

DINGO: And you, Jack.

MOGG: So have I.

DINGO: Gentian violet.

MOGG: I think it attracts the flies.

DINGO: Like cake.
MOGG: Don't make me laugh.
DINGO: I shall shortly piss gentian violet.
MOGG: Then piss some over me.
DINGO: The thing about fighting a desert war.
MOGG: We agreed not to talk about it.
DINGO: I must state it for them.
MOGG: Piss some over me because my sores are lifting up their flaming lips.
DINGO: The thing about fighting in the desert is that it is a clean war—without brutality. And clean limbed—without dishonourable actions on either side.
MOGG: They say.
DINGO: And there are no civilians.
MOGG: Except me—I'm a civilian.
DINGO: What am I then?
MOGG: Try as I may—I can't see you standing for a number eight bus picking your nose with the edge of your paper.
DINGO: Or barbarity.
MOGG: I've never stopped being a civilian.
DINGO: Or frightfulness.
MOGG: No refinements.
DINGO: I think you are a civilian.
MOGG: I can't deny that—I find the climate most exhilarating. . . .
DINGO: Characteristic of a civilian.
MOGG: You'll find the climate most exhilarating.
DINGO: Take for instance the shit beetle—a more exhilarative sight . . .
MOGG: And I find excitement bubbling within me . . .
DINGO: . . . you never shat.
MOGG: . . . at the nearness of the enemy.
DINGO: Characteristic of a civilian.

MOGG: Or a soldier.
DINGO: When did we last brew up?
MOGG: The inevitable brew up.
DINGO: Thumbs up.
MOGG: Desert fashion—the old brew up.
DINGO: You take the old benzina.
MOGG: Take the old sand.
DINGO: Take the old brew can.
MOGG: Sand.
DINGO: Benzina.
MOGG: And you take the old dixie.
DINGO: Water.
MOGG: In the old dixie.
DINGO: Benzina.
MOGG: On the old sand.
DINGO: Light the old benzina.

Flash. They've gone. A tank burns.

Smoke from the burning tank oils black across the sky. A TANKMAN *with goggles and white face skids into the hole with* MOGG *and* DINGO. *He is burning too—but he beats it out.*

Screams from the burning tank shrill through the low thudding battle noise. Inside the tank CHALKY WHITE *burns to death and screams.*

TANKY: I burned my hands.
DINGO: Your lot's over there.
TANKY: Oh yes?
DINGO: Back there—two hundred yards.
MOGG: I should go and report to three and fourpence.
DINGO: I shouldn't hang on here—you can do no good here.
TANKY: It's Chalky.

DINGO: It is?
MOGG: I should tell them that.
TANKY: He's in there.
DINGO: Yes—he is, isn't he?
TANKY: Look—tried to open his hatch. He couldn't open his hatch you see—it was glowing red hot all around his hatch—can you imagine his skin against that?
MOGG: I put my hand on a stove once.
DINGO: Silly bleeder.
TANKY: I burned my hands.
MOGG: I took all my hand off.
DINGO: What a stupid fartarsing thing to do.
TANKY: Pulling.
DINGO: Couldn't you put a bullet in him?
TANKY: I couldn't do that—he's a good lad.
MOGG: That's how I felt—I felt like chopping it off. . . . I felt as if the whole of my hand was flaming up—you know what I mean? I saw it flaming in bed for weeks after. . . .
TANKY: Shut up Chalky—belt up you bastard.
DINGO: That's it. Get it out of your system—you'll feel better.
MOGG: Burn—you bastard.
TANKY: I've got to get him out.
DINGO: He owe you money?
MOGG: He'll be all right when his brain goes.
TANKY: He'd do it for me.
MOGG: Maybe it's gone already.
TANKY: That's it—he'll not feel anything will he?
DINGO: Roll on death.
TANKY: It's a clean way to go though isn't it?
MOGG: The wogs prefer it.
DINGO: They'd do their nuts if you offered to bury them tidy.

MOGG: They prefer it.

DINGO: He must have been a tough bloke.

MOGG: They're all toughies in the Lancers aren't they boy?

DINGO: I admire it.

MOGG: I wish I could be the same.

TANKY: I ought to try to get him out.

DINGO: I should go and tell your C.O.

MOGG: Two hundred yards due south—turn left at the Rifleman's grave and right again where you see the flies. . . .

DINGO: Don't poke about—it'll only depress you.

MOGG: We all come to it.

DINGO: That's where you'll find him—with any luck you'll catch Starlight too. . . .

TANKY: I can't listen—I can't listen.

MOGG: He wouldn't want you to.

DINGO: He'd want you to go on.

TANKY: Can't you do something—shoot him—blow it up shoot him?

CHALKY *stops screaming.*

DINGO: There.

MOGG: That's better for you.

TANKY: I tried to pull him out didn't I?

MOGG: Back there—figures two hundred or so back there turn left at the Rifleman. . . .

TANKY: He brewed up didn't he?

They put on steel helmets with red bands and Military Police brassards.

DINGO: Right—move on trooper—rejoin your unit.

MOGG: . . . and right again where you see the flies.

DINGO: Battle police.

MOGG: Rejoin your unit.
TANKY: Battle Police...?
DINGO: Royal Corps of...
MOGG: You'll find your RHQ due south....
TANKY: Thanks.
DINGO: Our job.
MOGG: We know where everyone is.
DINGO: Any time.
MOGG: We got you up here.
DINGO: Yes—if it wasn't for us, Jack, you'd still be swanning about the desert looking for a battle.
MOGG: Due south.
TANKY: Thanks.
DINGO: Remember me to the colonel.
TANKY: If you see Chalky....
MOGG: We'll bury him.
DINGO: Only we won't see him—we don't get any action.
TANKY: That's him again.

Another scream starts.

MOGG: We promise you it's not.
DINGO: You can take it from us, mate—that's foreign.
TANKY: I can't bear it.
MOGG: No. It's not Chalky.
DINGO: He thinks it's Chalky.
MOGG: Look—it's foreign. No British Squaddie goes on like that.
DINGO: Go out and finish him if you like.
TANKY: No—let the bastard scream.
MOGG: He'll belt up shortly. (*He does.*) There—these fucking Eyeties haven't got the stamina.
TANKY: Funny that.
DINGO: It wasn't.
TANKY: I don't know how you do it.

MOGG: Due south two hundred yards. . . .
TANKY: It's Chalky.
DINGO: You tell them. . . .
TANKY: . . . get him on the blood wagon—quack'll fix him up, won't he? Left at the Rifleman's grave?
MOGG: . . . right again at the flies. . . .
DINGO: Don't mess about with the flies. . . .

TANKY *goes—bent double and running.*

MOGG: . . . straight up the minefield.
DINGO: It's a clean way to go.
MOGG: How do you know the difference?
DINGO: What—between screams?
MOGG: Yes—you can't tell one from the other. You were taking the piss.
DINGO: No.
MOGG: They all sound the same to me, mate.
DINGO: No.
MOGG: Go on.
DINGO: Tell you what—next one . . . half a sheet—right?
MOGG: You're on.
DINGO: Eyes down.

They're gone. A desert battle.

A NAVIGATING OFFICER *navigates his battalion walking in front of nobody—his eyes tight on the compass he's holding. He waves nobody on . . . nobody follows him. He stops—takes a bearing with commendable courage and waves again to nobody behind him.*

DINGO *peeks over the top.*

DINGO: Half a sheet the next one to scream is clean, dry and slightly upperclass white English.
MOGG: You can't tell all that.

DINGO: Half a sheet.
MOGG: That was him then—going across.
DINGO: But I don't know do I? I don't know as how he'll scream.
MOGG: You can be dead certain can't you?
DINGO: Now how can I? There's a lot of luck.
MOGG: Bloody twister. If you've seen him.
DINGO: Scrub it.
MOGG: No—I'll let it stand.
DINGO: Scrub it.
MOGG: No—but it's nigh on a dead cert if you've seen him gone for a shit with a rug wrapped round him.
DINGO: I said scrub it—scrub it.
MOGG: You only guess anyway.
DINGO: I know.
MOGG: Down.

They down. The NAVIGATING OFFICER *navigates his way to their hole and stops.*

NAVIGATING OFFICER: This is Green.
DINGO: No.
MOGG: You mean this is Blue.
NAVIGATING OFFICER: No—this is Green.
MOGG: Blue.
DINGO: Hello Two One Able—we are at Blue—two one able Over.
MOGG: Hello Two One Able—say again—Over.
NAVIGATING OFFICER: Green.
DINGO: Hello Two One Able—I say again we are at Blue —Two One Able Over.
NAVIGATING OFFICER: No.
MOGG: Two One Able—Roger—How far from Green—Over.
DINGO: Two One Able—figures four miles—Over.

MOGG: Two One Able—Roger—Out.

NAVIGATING OFFICER: You're wrong.

DINGO: Blue.

MOGG: Blue.

NAVIGATING OFFICER: Green.

DINGO: Blue.

MOGG: Blue.

NAVIGATING OFFICER (*courageously*): Green.

DINGO: Listen—blue.

MOGG: All right, Jack? Blue.

NAVIGATING OFFICER: I know Green—when I see it.

DINGO: Blue.

MOGG: Blue.

DINGO: We know blue when we see it.

MOGG: Hello Two One Able—Position—Two One Able Over.

DINGO: Hello Two One Able—Position—Wait . . . Wait —Out.

MOGG: Blue.

NAVIGATING OFFICER: Ask them if they know where Green is.

DINGO: Hello Two One Able—Position—Blue—I say again Blue . . . where is Green? Two One Able—Over.

MOGG: Two One Able—Left at the Rifleman's grave —Over.

DINGO: Two One Able—Roger—Out.

MOGG: Sir.

NAVIGATING OFFICER: I know. Left at the Rifleman's grave. I know—I'm a navigating officer.

DINGO: Then you would know, wouldn't you, sir.

MOGG: The thing is, sir—we're not sure. . . .

DINGO: Sappers, sir—we was asked to move to blue and set up a water point, sir.

MOGG: . . . we're not sure we should start pumping or not, sir. . . .

DINGO: Point is—the whole army'll be looking for blue. . .

NAVIGATING OFFICER: This is Blue.

DINGO: Sir.

MOGG: Then we should set up our water point here, sir?

NAVIGATING OFFICER: Set up your water point here. At Blue.

DINGO: Sir.

NAVIGATING OFFICER: I am moving to Green.

MOGG: Due south two hundred yards, left. . . .

NAVIGATING OFFICER: . . . I know—at the Rifleman's grave —I'm a navigating officer. . . .

DINGO: Right again at the flies. . . .

The NAVIGATING OFFICER *goes. Eyes on compass and very daring upright posture.*

MOGG: Straight up the minefield.

DINGO: I was wrong.

MOGG: About the next one.

DINGO: It was a mistake anyone could make.

MOGG: Half a sheet.

DINGO: Men's lives.

MOGG: What of it?

DINGO: Don't you find it ghoulish betting money on men's lives?

MOGG: My leash it then.

DINGO: Typical civilian. It's like half a sheet on whether Jesus . . . isn't it?

MOGG: Declare it null.

DINGO: No. No—I'll pay up. I want to pay up. I want to see the disgusting ghoulish way your tongue comes out to look at the money.

MOGG: I don't bet on men's lives. I bet on their screams.

DINGO: Torturer.
MOGG: It's only whether or not—that's all. It's not pressing the tit . . . pulling the pin, trigger, bayonet out. Anyway Jesus was a foregone conclusion. . . . I wouldn't have had anything on him.
DINGO: Here.
MOGG: I don't want it.
DINGO: Pick it up off the floor.
MOGG: Bend down?
DINGO: Pick it up.
MOGG: I'm sick and bloody tired of you. I want to get back to being frightened. I want to get back to the lads and shit myself at shadows with the lads and run slack arsed through the dust pointing my bondhook for ripping. I haven't had a good toss off in months.

I'm full up to here with dirty water sit and scratch my navel. I want to stick it in and think it's gone. I've not nothing to inspire me.
DINGO: You don't.
MOGG: No—I don't. But I want you to know that I'm not satisfied with the life we're leading.
DINGO: Do you think I am?
MOGG: It's different for you—in'it?
DINGO: You're starting.
MOGG: Well—it is.
DINGO: How's it different for me then?
MOGG: Well I'm differently placed aren't I? It's a well-known fact it's different for regular swaddies.
DINGO: How's it a well-known fact.
MOGG: Due to it being your trade in'it?

You're a soldier by trade en't you. You don't find it like we do—like having it off do you?

I find it exhilarating. . . .
DINGO: You're a fucking farceur.

MOGG: Get in Joseph—it's your birthday.
DINGO: Make tracks then.
MOGG: Coooooooor—get down Fido you pointer dog you.
DINGO: Make tracks.
MOGG: Oh yes.
DINGO: Only don't come back to me all minus and ask me to bandage you up . . . don't come back to me all red at the seams and ask me to push it back.

You think I don't get these feelings? Don't think I don't get these feelings, Mogg. I'm just as randy as you are, Mogg. I have a good brisk run around the battlefield and make do with my mirage.

MOGG: She gets on my tits.
DINGO: Shouldn't you be getting on hers?
MOGG: I'm sick and tired of my bleeding mirage.
DINGO: You should have thought of that.

Shouldn't you be getting on hers? shouldn't you?

MOGG: You can't be blamed for your mirage.
DINGO: I can blame you.
MOGG: How can you? It's an act of God, in'it?
DINGO: Don't bring him into it—God's a wog—he wants to get back where he came from.
MOGG: See how it goes. We can always come back.
DINGO: I've been dreaming on and off—while the fleas leave go my knackers on and off. I had a dream last night/the night before—they're all the same, cold, black—it was the night before.
MOGG: Give it another try. Let's see how it goes.
DINGO: Shit in it a minute, will you?

This dream. . . . It was me and you standing stark bollocks naked as the day we was born, holding hands together under the stars. . . .

No, it wasn't. I romanticise.

This dream—it was you and me scrambling up the side of sand, in a wadi, sand that slid under us boots to show like bones out of legs—pieces of blokes . . . and you'd scarpered. I looked all over the shop for you—you'd gone up to Annie's room, you had.

MOGG: I'm proud of you.

DINGO: Mickey—I wouldn't tell a lie. No—I tell a lie. . . .

MOGG: We can come back.

DINGO: This dream—one of us.

MOGG: One of us. What about 'one of us'?

DINGO: That's it. Just one of us.

MOGG: What?

DINGO: Which. More like which?

MOGG: Why can't I change my mirage. . . ?

DINGO: Why can't you change your mind?

MOGG: I can—I've changed my mind—I'm stopping here.

DINGO: I'll believe that when I see your mirage.

MOGG: Here. You seen his? They seen yours Dingo?

DINGO: If they were in last night they have—haven't they? I'm satisfied.

MOGG: His mirage is an old bag.

Here—her teeth. Now then . . . her teeth so rotten they've marched into open order, separated up. They lean . . . now then, they lean in her stinking mouth, forwards, right and left, front and rear, advance and retire.

Yellow streaked gravestones, see—sinking with the drop of decay underneath—round at the edges—worn smooth by tongues, birds, paws, cocks, crusts, hands, rain and tools.

Up the far end of the cemetery, where they put the coke and lean on their shovels, brooms for the leaves, kids from the houses play off the wall and on to the stone—goods and bad—Jerries and British.

Mourners taken short, look round fast round the back of head, in a hurry to get their sharp, stone fresh, new sawed, aren't we glad we gave Dad a granite . . . mourners quick piss on them.

And so do I.

DINGO: I'm satisfied. (*He lies face to the hot overhead sun. He has his hands behind his head.*)

MOGG: He's satisfied.

DINGO: Don't mock.

MOGG: Here. Her tits—her tits hang low as to swing her ammo pouches would rub them now—and when they swing as they swing, she stinks up through the neck-hole of her blanket style White Cliffs of Dover suit—mingles with the breath air lumping up from her guts—stirs the grass growing yellow between the gravestones . . . the yellow grass on her tongue, chin, hanging from her scabby nostrils.

Hey Limey—don't kiss that girl. . . .

DINGO: It's question of taste—in'it?

MOGG: I'd rot in my lips.

My lips would ulcerate—just forced to stand chatting her toe to toe.

DINGO: Depends on what you want.

Now then—him. His mirage is all stories. You look and shift in your seat for the heat—I scald my balls . . . I'll grant you that—only it's all stories.

His mirage is stories. Her long blonde hair hangs down her back . . . is stories.

MOGG: I'm satisfied.

DINGO: What you ticking for then?

MOGG: I'm not ticking—I'm just not satisfied.

DINGO: Don't say you are then.

MOGG: My mirage is all stories—her long blonde hair is stories. Her big alabaster blue subtle veined breasts is stories—her soft wave of honey milk breath is stories.

DINGO: In soft covers.

MOGG: Scrape your mind for stories in every kind of cover —soft, hard, plain brown not to reveal, silent and musical. . . .

They come up coloured.
They come up described.
They come up blueprint to the last short hair.
They don't come up perforated that's all.
You ever tried to stuff a story?

DINGO: Mine's no story. She may be a scrubber—but she's warm and smells and you touch her . . .

MOGG: Not me—with yours.

DINGO: . . . mine's real.

MOGG: Mine's a big woman.

DINGO: But she does you no good.

MOGG: Once I thought I'd got it—it was a real day for sun on the back of the head and mirages were leaping about like kids on the beach—just take your pick of skin—between her legs I found a breech block and when I pulled her arm the breech came, started to slide and heavy on the grease opened a chink. I thought chunk chunch it'll drop—just a pull more and it'll drop open . . . black red, not white walled.

They always open—take up the slack and jerk hard when you feel the weight and hear the grease film toffee . . . open the breech—and loaded you cry —thuchunk your balled fist is smooth as silk lifted up. . . .

I pulled on that arm forever and no breech would open.

DINGO: All stories.

MOGG: All smooth.

DINGO: All hard centres.
MOGG: Don't tell me you find joy.
DINGO: Every time.
MOGG: If we go. . . .
DINGO: If we go—there's still mirages in the afternoon.
MOGG: No—not that . . . if we go—what do you mean "one of us"—what you said?
DINGO: Christ, I sweat.
MOGG: The sun's up.
DINGO: Christ, I shiver.
MOGG: Come up, sun. . . .
DINGO: The ball in my head is red.
MOGG: Come up, sun, on the small of my back . . .
DINGO: The sun is so scalding it's white.

The ball in my head is white and it shimmers from left frontal lobe to right frontal lobe—spit on a stove. . . .

Speech is slow from dry mouth and big tongues that fit the bore of the mouth tight as a cartridge. The wonder is that they talk at all with this cartridge hot and expanded after firing tight in their black mouth breeches.

MOGG: My time.

This time—I'll mirage up a belly dancer—Farouk Farouk bollocks on a hook—belly dancer with navel ten feet and longer deep in the belly stretching here to wherever.

DINGO: I'm still satisfied.
MOGG: Ten feet deep. Fill that in.
DINGO: Ambition.
MOGG: And she do—I'll take up my bondhook and fight.
DINGO: And you do, and you do . . . I had this dream . . . one of us.

Music. Not connected music—just wild notes till they come together for a belly dance tune.

TANKY *arrives—same state.*

They lie flat. Arms out flat in the now hard overhead sun.

TANKY *carries* CHALKY.

CHALKY *has been burned to death in a sitting position. He is black charred thin as a black dried in the sun long dead bean. His arms are bent over his pin head to open his hatch. Bits of still intact khaki drill flap from the crook of his elbows, crutch, and around his ankles.*

He sits on TANKY*'s knee. While* TANKY *talks to him . . .*

TANKY: Drunk again.

DINGO *and* MOGG *flip flap their hands and groan.*

Chalky's pissed again.

Will you rattle should I shake you? Or will you slosh? Remember the leaves all had water on them Chalky my son/my old mucker, clambering back into where was it? You pissed yourself at the water on the laurels . . . water you cried—tasted of metal, soot. It was really humorous. And you sat down with me laughing wet through pulled by the tab of my jacket down to your bum in mud . . . in my ear while my booted foot swayed to the laugh of my belly . . . to the guard—stand to the guard—I'll wake the bloody guard . . . bring out the guard in the rain—stand to the guard by the seaside.

You shouted.

You said.

Stand to the Blackpool Tower guard.

For there are spies up the Blackpool Tower watching us wash the water up from Ireland between our—stinking dirt and sock fluff between the ranks—military toes.

You were aggressive.

This beer's watered down, this beer's adulterated with pig's piddle. It's all we can get now Jack.

Try it for on your hair a tonic.

Splash splash—up through the leaves on your face.

DINGO: 99 change hands.

MOGG: Don't care if I do go blind.

The sun is not so hot now. DINGO *and* MOGG *sit/stand up as the music jerk fades. They rub their crutches,* DINGO *happy,* MOGG *ruefully.*

MOGG: Again.

DINGO: Did you get him in?

TANKY: I got him out.

MOGG: That's it. . . .

They notice the proud, grinning TANKY.

. . . Now for the other.

DINGO: What you got there?

MOGG: Where did you get that?

DINGO: You.

TANKY: I got him out.

DINGO: You've been picking up things on the battlefield.

TANKY: Chalky.

MOGG: Oh my God—get it dug in.

DINGO: This sun.

MOGG: Brings out the worst—you'll have it very bad if it turns.

DINGO: I'm disgusted.

You tramp feet raw looking for a bleeding place where you don't have to cuddle corpses so as you don't have to lose all sense. . . .

Keep some sense of fitness. . . .

MOGG: Arrives on a gari.

DINGO: Get it dug in.

What's the matter with you? You puggled? You're puggled—can't you take simple direct instructions?

Don't concern you, Jack.

Take it somewheres else.

MOGG: Left at the Rifleman's grave. . . .

DINGO: He's been there—you been there?

MOGG: He's been there, has he?

Notice an officer looking for Green?

DINGO: Notice an sergeant searching for heroifycation?

TANKY: Chalky.

I got him out, see. I told you I'd get him out—I wouldn't let him down.

While they are talking the COMIC *sets up a booth down away from them. It is getting dark and when he finishes erecting his one-man stage he turns on two lights.*

DINGO: You ain't been there then, have you?

MOGG: A thought's just struck me. . . .

DINGO: They've had it cleared. Well, you're not the only one—that thought struck me.

Who do you reckon he is anyway.

MOGG: . . . they could have cleared it—or they could have stepped on them all.

That could have happened.

DINGO: Oh yes—what sort of minefield is that then—it might be your idea of a minefield—it's not mine. . . .

You can't call a minefield a minefield unless it's like currants in a cake—every now and then a bleeding great sultana . . . that's a minefield.

You didn't walk through that.

MOGG: He'd have a bloody crutch if he did.

DINGO: Too true.

They look at TANKY, *who smiles.*

And who do you reckon he is?

TANKY: Chalky.

MOGG: That. . . . ?

DINGO: O yes . . . highly likely.

How do you make that out then? You had a good butchers at it? No—well go on—have a good shufti. Emotions apart—have a good hard shufti at that pipe cleaner you got sitting on your lap.

MOGG: Bears no relation.

DINGO: That?

MOGG: Bears no relation to the British Soldier.

DINGO: None whatever.

MOGG: Just doesn't compare.

TANKY: I couldn't leave him there . . . for all and sundry —I surely couldn't loose him down could I? I had to see you were all right . . .

DINGO: Stone me.

MOGG: He's talking to it.

DINGO: Like it was something.

TANKY: . . . didn't I Chalky?

Well—he only lives up the road.

COMIC: Leave the first three rows for the officers will you?

DINGO *and* MOGG *notice the* COMIC *for the first time—they leave* TANKY *and walk over to the stage.* MOGG *is happy—almost excited.* DINGO *is agitated.*

DINGO: What's this, George?

COMIC: We entertain you.

Taraaaaaaaaaaaa. A chord of music splashes—or a drum roll and cymbal crash.

Stand Easy and let yourself go—it's the Tails up and Lick 'em show.

Just keep the first three rows for the officers will you—I thank you.

MOGG: I thank you.

DINGO: Don't laugh—don't encourage him.

MOGG: I like a laugh.

DINGO: I don't mind the occasional lost, stolen, or bleeding strayed half cock swaddie—I don't mind the odd pig ignorant leading his band of happy heroes. . . .

MOGG: Tit show is it?

DINGO: We've seen it George.

MOGG: I ain't seen it.

DINGO: You've seen it. Saw it yesterday.

COMIC: What you think of the show then? Mind you I've played Green before—I always go down very well at Green. . . .

MOGG: Leg show is it?

COMIC: Brought the house down I did with my "Man does not live by Bread alone" gag. You like that one . . . it's a lovely story. Always goes down well before a killing match.

MOGG: Tit show is it?

DINGO: You can't play Green again can you?

COMIC: Oh no—mind you it's a nice theatre.
TANKY: Hey—Chalky's pissed again. (*He walks* CHALKY *in front of him—makes him sway about like a drunk.*)
COMIC: A vent—lovely act. Always goes down well.
DINGO: Sorry. We've booked him—ventriloquist.
COMIC: Double booking? No—can't be. Where's this then?
DINGO: Green.
COMIC: Can't be.
DINGO: That's right in'it?
MOGG: Is it a Tit show?
NAVIGATING OFFICER: This is Blue.
COMIC: There you are—I've played Blue too many times for that—no fly space. Mind you it's an easy show.
TANKY: Chalky likes a good laugh—don't you mate? (*He answers himself as* CHALKY*—a high-pitched pursed lip voice.*)
CHALKY: Too bloody true.
DINGO: No sir—this is Green sir.
NAVIGATING OFFICER: Very humorous. . . .
COMIC: Very nice sir.
TANKY: No—it's only me really.
COMIC: Very nice.
DINGO: Because we had him last night sir—very good show . . . that "Man does not live by Bread alone" gag—been pissing ourselves all day over that. . . .
COMIC: Can you do the old drink of water business?

The sky darkens. DINGO *stands in the middle of the stage and shouts.*

DINGO: This is Green.
NAVIGATING OFFICER: No.
MOGG: He's a navigating officer.
NAVIGATING OFFICER: This is Blue . . .
MOGG: Where they have the tit shows . . .

NAVIGATING OFFICER: Where they have the water point.

DINGO: This is Green—this is Green.

NAVIGATING OFFICER: You want Green?

MOGG: I can help you out there . . .

Two hundred yards due south—left at the . . .

NAVIGATING OFFICER: Pull yourself together.

DINGO: Green.

NAVIGATING OFFICER: Have you got a map? Right—figures two hundred yards due south—left at the Rifleman's grave. . . .

Do you think your officers—I am an officer you know—I'm a navigating officer, lead on, navigating officer, do you think your officers don't know one stretch of desert from another?

DINGO: Green.

NAVIGATING OFFICER: Sand happy. Green—I do know where Green is you know—we all know where Green is—right? Green was won after heavy fighting and navigating. Green will go down like Longstep and Knightsbridge, I would have preferred it something catchy like silly mid-on, or underarm ridge, but mustn't bellyache. Green is etched deep and honourably on the hearts of gallant men who died that there might be a chapter headed Green, blazoned in letters of gold on their regiment's colour is Green. Green cost dear. Green is two hundred yards due south—turn left at the Rifleman's grave and right again at the flies. . . .

MOGG: Don't poke around with the flies.

NAVIGATING OFFICER: Only lower your morale.

MOGG: . . . straight up the minefield. (*He smiles at* DINGO.) Bum titty bum titty bum bum bum.

COMIC: It's the Tails Up and Lick 'em Show. (*He stands*

on his stage and opens the show—music Blaaaaarts out of Nowhere.)

MOGG, TANKY *and the* NAVIGATING OFFICER *sit on the floor in front of the stage.* DINGO *hovers separate.*

DINGO: What sort of minefield is that. Minefield. . . .
MOGG: Hurrah, Hurrah.
TANKY: Hurrah, Hurrah.
COMIC: That's all right mother—plenty of room in the stalls. . . . (DINGO *sits.*)
Don't mind me—I'm an idle abortionist—I specialise in struggling actresses who didn't.
TANKY: Didn't what?
COMIC: Struggle. At ease, Colonel. He's suffering from bottle fatigue. . . . We were married by candle light but she just got on my wick. . . .

The stage gets darker and darker until there is only light on the COMIC*'s small stage. The heroes have arrived carrying their exhausted Colonel.* DINGO *doesn't laugh. The* COMIC *puts on a beret with two badges in it.*

COMIC: My first encounter with Rommel was of great interest—luckily I had time to sort out the mess and the Jock columns and get some sort of willingness from below due to grip from above. I don't smoke and I don't drink but I do grip and I did see him off. No trouble there and the ball's in my court which I won when it was his service . . . now it is my service—the score standing at one-love . . . Talking of love did you hear the one about the gippo bint with the pieyard, as they call their bow-wows. A pissyarsed Digger jig-a-jigs the sister out of bounds one night—say Sheila what's the dog for? Something new Johnny.

HERO DIGGER: Why what you got? Leprosy?

COMIC: Two pounds Johnny, and a pound for the dog, Johnny, what? He licks the back of your neck—just on paradise and bells and green waves lapping the timeless ocean—came the raid . . . redcaps like thick on the ground like so much blood . . . the bint gets a belting, a redcap and a dose of clap hands for daddy—the digger gets jankers, a runny nose and a thing about pieyards . . . the dog? He got his licence endorsed. Yap. Yap.

Thank you. Thank you.

Welfare. . . . Man does not live by bread alone. . . . The British Soldier properly led responds to a challenge and not to welfare benefits. He will do anything you ask of him so long as he gets his letters, the local rag and, curiously enough, plenty of tea. . . .

TANKY: Can you hear me, mother?

A burst of spandau.

COMIC: He then likes to know, with his tea, what, just what, is going on in the killing ground, and what, just what, you require him to do. He gets anxious if his home town is bombed, smashed, squeezed to powder and paint, signal red, and he can't get news about his wife, his girl and his children. . . .

A burst of spandau.

HERO COLONEL: That is too much. First bit of relaxation I've had in months.

SCOT HERO: Is you bothering you, Colonel?

HERO COLONEL: Without more ado this gentleman of Scotland—for he was a real gentleman although born in humble and disgusting circumstances and twice convicted of rape with a blunt instrument, once convicted of the Gorbals on a Saturday belongs to me, belongs to me . . . he slides into the night.

SCOT HERO *slides into the night.*

Saying: 'Is yon bothering ye at all Colonel Harry sir.' He knew I hadn't had a bit of relaxation in weeks.

MOGG: Did you see that?

DINGO: I saw it.

COMIC: Talking of children. My wife had twins . . . the first time I've been paid twice for the one performance. . . .

For Chats, Nobby, Winger and Bummer of K block the Knightsbridge Box from Wren Berker and all the other elastic bottom and tops. . . .

Music of the Vera Lynn kind in the background as part of the general mush.

DINGO: For my wife who cries, don't cry. Get out and drop your drawers—loosen your blackouts, don't tell me, but let the top of your head go whirl with the stir of Churchill's cigar . . . for my wife who cries—don't cry.

A burst of accordion music.

COMIC: Are you being rude?

Another burst of accordion music—somewhere someone is getting ready to play the accordion. It annoys the HERO COLONEL, *who gets to his feet and shouts in exasperation that he regrets as soon as his outburst is over.*

HERO COLONEL: Oh damn. Oh damn it. This is the first bit of relaxation in months.

The doughty DIGGER HERO *strides forward and says:*

DIGGER: Hey cobber, my old sport, digger colonel for a pom . . . is that wop bothering you with his flaming squeezebox? No Job you cobber.

HERO COLONEL: Calls me cobber. . . .

DIGGER: Cobber.

HERO COLONEL: Digger.

DIGGER: Cobber.

"Waltzing Matilda" behind speech.

HERO COLONEL: With that fine contempt for rank, danger and full of sheer bloody guts and determination that makes him such a fine soldier and endears him to us all . . . calls me. . . .

MOGG: Sport.

HERO COLONEL: Sport. The Digger strides head up into the night.

MOGG: Sport.

HERO COLONEL: Sport.

MOGG: Calls me sport.

DINGO: What are you looking for? You, Mogg, I'm talking to you.

COMIC: Man does not live by bread alone. The troops must be brought up to a state of wild enthusiasm before the operation begins. Give our gallant Scot a burst of wild enthusiasm.

The SCOTS HERO *is back. He sits down.*

DINGO: He willna bother you any mair, Colonel.

COMIC: I am two hundred per cent fit. I do not believe, no you can't expect troops to win battles unless they are in top-hole condition, top-hole.

DINGO: Arsehole.

COMIC: Bellyaching will not be tolerated . . . when I first saw bellyaching . . . I knew that the Commander did not have . . . his finger on the spiritual pulse of his men . . . "if I do the two-mile run, I do the two-mile run, sir". . . . He stood before me and said . . . "but if I do the two-mile run sir I will die . . . my doctor says I will die" . . . he came to me and bellyached in front of me—no binge "I will die" . . . then I said, I told him . . . "I would rather you did the two-mile run, Colonel, and died now, Colonel, than that you should die later just when we are about to have a battle, it is dashed inconvenient to have officers dying before a battle" . . . he did the run and as far as I know he did not die.

NAVIGATING OFFICER: I'm a navigating officer. I do a deal of running hup hup.

COMIC: There, there, that.

Accordion is starting into a hymn when it is stopped as if it were strangled.

I do not believe troops can succeed unless they are infected with that optimism that comes from well being.

NAVIGATING OFFICER: Hup hup.

HERO COLONEL: . . . with the light of battle in their eyes and wanting to kill the enemy . . . no commander can inspire or lead even single units without a proper sense of religious truth . . . bottled up in men are great emotional forces. . . .

The DIGGER *comes back and tosses the broken accordion at the* COLONEL*'s feet.* MOGG *is very impressed. The* COLONEL *is now full of binge. He has lost his fatigue and combs his hair.*

Be sure that the fine spiritual purpose which inspires us all is clearly expounded to one and all.

Men are the raw material with which a commander has to deal . . . he must give them an outlet for the great emotional forces bottled in them, in us all . . . an outlet which is positive and constructive, the thought of which warms the heart and excites the imagination. If you can gain their confidence and their trust, and they feel that their best interests lie in your hands, you have in your possession a priceless asset, and the greatest achievements become possible.

The HERO COLONEL *goes to the front of his men. He stands against the low rumbling barrage that is light in the sky. There are Very lights in the sky. The* SIKH HERO *goes to fetch him a cup of tea. He gets the mug and walks slowly across the sand so that it shall not be spilled.*

There is a bright gleam that has caught the helmets of our soldiers, it flickers on their bayonets, it laps fiery as brandy in the vessels of their bodies. Eyes jerk and are straightened . . . muscle slides to will of brain. Gone is the evil wasting mist which clogs and clouds so that one's own hand is another man's. Gone is the lifting drunken balloon of tiredness which takes mind aloft to view an empty shell of bloodied khaki filth, your body, your familiar splay of feet, your machinery grinding spit and sand, your sad flutter of hand at thigh. . . .

Gone. You know you are a man.

You know your feet will march on stones that do not shift, you feel your head will watch and command . . . you have peace and you have balance . . . there is once more . . . there is brightness, for one more time there is steady shining brightness. The light is on our soldiers and they spark in its gleam, for they are steel.

They are together welded to a STEEL.

The COMIC *packs up his booth and switches the lights off. Most of the light comes from the gunflashes now and the barrage noise grows. The* SIKH *is blown to bits.*

HERO COLONEL: Fetch me another mug of tea, someone.
COMIC: I was in the last one.
MOGG: That's it. You coming? See that? You coming? Fetch me another mug of tea. . . .
DINGO: You're a bleeding hero, Micky Mogg.
NAVIGATING OFFICER: I'm a. . . .
TANKY: I'd like to go, but I can't leave Chalky.
DINGO: That's not Chalky.
TANKY: It is Chalky.
DINGO: No, it's not. Look, look out there. You see faces . . . ladies. . . .
TANKY: They've come to see Chalky and me being brave.
DINGO: No.
TANKY: Evening.
DINGO: No. Mothers down there. And wives and daughters and sisters . . . Roger so far?
TANKY: Roger . . . and I want to thank you all for being such a wonderful audience to play to. . . .
DINGO: Mothers. Seen their sons go off with lust and blood in their eyes—mud on their boots . . . you know what? They used to wave the boats off.
TANKY: Really—I want you to know from the bottom of my heart . . . it's been a privilege to play to you tonight. Stop on, you'll hear some lovely singing.

DINGO: Used to wave the boats off full of waving sons—husbands, fathers, brothers doing positive and constructive work . . . Roger so far?

TANKY: Roger—as one of our finest soldiers said he said "man does not live by bread alone."

DINGO: They're down there watching.

TANKY: Mothers.

DINGO: Yes.

TANKY: Say hello, Chalky.

DINGO: No, it's grotesque—and it's not Chalky.

Do you think we'd make a mistake like that?

Do you think that black, burnt up, high in the sun stinking charred old toothy old jerk of raw material is a British swaddie do you?

Do you think we'd risk offending every mother here tonight with unlikely looking material. Highly upset they'd be. That's enemy. People out there lost their dear ones—that's enemy. No British soldier dies like that. That's enemy. You won't find a photograph, a statue, a painting of a British soldier like that.

TANKY: He died well, did Chalky.

DINGO: That Chalky? Never. They wouldn't have it. They'd be up in arms if they thought that was a killed on the field of honour green. Cross their legs and shout no more.

TANKY: He died to rid the world of evil—what about the concentration camps?

DINGO: We don't know about those yet.

TANKY: What about the Jews?

DINGO: We don't know about the Jews yet.

TANKY: He died for spiritual purpose.

DINGO: I heard him. Gott mit uns.

TANKY: He died for . . . he died anyway.

DINGO: Yes he died because he couldn't get out. You've

been taken in . . . that, not like that did he die, evil enemy die like that. You've been taken in . . . like Micky Mogg there panting to join the colours. He's just been taken in . . . because he hasn't done it.

That you have there is a Kraut . . . you can tell by his brutal chin.

TANKY: Uuuuuuugh. Bloody Kraut.

He throws CHALKY *away . . . as he does the* COLONEL HERO *drops raised hand and bagpipes, smoke, barrage, Alamein.*

DINGO: The best place to be in a battle is in the thick of it only with your head down and a look of eager blood-lust in your eyes. Better still if you look confident and if you know where you are you can direct others to where you're not.

They hop after the others. The battle ends. The stage is empty except for the COMIC *and the* HERO SCOT, *sitting still clutching his chest. The* COMIC *goes over to him.*

COMIC: What can I say, eh? Well, you've heard it like you've heard most of them before, still goes down well, though, usually only when I laugh. Yes. Have you had your eyes checked? No, they've always been brown. Now, did you hear the one about the wee Jock who inadvertently stood on an S mine? On his way back to the R.A.P. holding his bloody piece in his both hands he met his colonel who said "I'll stop this self abuse."

No, only when I laugh.

SCOTS HERO *starts to chuckle, and as he does so he coughs up blood. Blackout.*

SCOTS HERO *starts to chuckle.*

Act Two

Scene One

A Prison Camp.

For other ranks British. DINGO *and* TANKY *are here. They are here somewhere in the looping lethal wire. The wire is on frames dropped in and gets smaller and tighter as it recedes up stage. So that the effect is of barbed wire stretching, fiddle string taut—looping in characteristic whorls—as far as the eye of a prisoner can see.*

There is room between the frames for movement. Searchlights pluck the wires and the wind makes the sound. Shreds of clothing and skin perhaps feathers are seen to jerk a little. Some of the shreds are pyjama striped. But they don't concern us.

The searchlights converge on an open space down stage and go out one by one. Until a small bulb dangling centre of the light circle that will be—is switched on and in the wide diffusion of light we see TANKY *and* DINGO. *In ragged uniform and greatcoats. And in a small boxing ring with an apron to it on the same slightly raised level.*

DINGO *and* TANKY *stand together holding hands—*

when they start talking they walk round in ever increasing circles.

But they start standing still.

DINGO: In a cell.
TANKY: And me—I'm in a cell.
DINGO: In a room.
TANKY: And me—I'm in this room.
DINGO: Are you going to repeat everything?
TANKY: I'm excited. (*And he blinks excited—making faces for laughs.*) It's the first time I've been captured.
DINGO: If you're going to repeat everything I say—this cell is going to get overcrowded.

They start walking round.

TANKY: What I like is the peace.
DINGO: If you go on like that my eardrums will give way.
TANKY: And the quiet and the time to do nothing.
DINGO: Not to mention the overheating.

They pass and DINGO *pushes* TANKY.

TANKY: Don't.

They stop and look at each other. Grinning happily.

DINGO: I will if you make the room mess or whatever overcrowded.
TANKY: I won't.
DINGO: See you don't.

Round again.

DINGO: This room is wooden stout construction form timbers from the Black Forest hard as a very hard prussian blue. Steel. And locked at night by a padlock made in Sheffield that used to clop in the hasp of tank side bin perhaps or rum ration cupboard. Strong.

TANKY: They have a bit of trouble opening it in the morning.

DINGO: A difficult padlock that often doesn't open first go.

TANKY: Wants some oil.

They lean back on the ropes arms outside.

DINGO: It's had some from the black on it.

TANKY: Good oil.

DINGO: It is good oil.

TANKY: They shouldn't waste good oil on us.

DINGO: No. What it is—it's bag happy like us.

They start round again coming inwards and tighter and faster as TANKY *gets a little frightened.*

TANKY: I'm bomb happy and bag happy.

DINGO: Dogs—listen!

They stop and listen. A DOG *howls—and it makes* TANKY *shiver.*

Dogs—big black and barking Adolf Hitler.

TANKY: Outside—they're outside.

DINGO: Pad round the room, hut, mess, or whatever.

TANKY: They are outside.

DINGO: I think that's clear enough.

TANKY: Yes.

DINGO: They wouldn't be inside.

TANKY: Are they not trained?

DINGO: Of course they're trained—highly trained—best trained dogs in the world are on a German leash.

TANKY: That's all right then—they can come in then. (*Brave.*)

DINGO: Trained to kill.

TANKY: Outside.

They stand close together holding hands.

I thought we'd left all that—there. I thought we'd finished with all that.

DINGO: Outside.

TANKY: Highly trained.

DINGO: To kill kriegies.

TANKY: Oh well. (*Relief.*)

They start widening out again.

DINGO: You're a kriegie.

TANKY (*stops*): When I was a nip bobbly knees that couldn't pass a wall without drawing blood from scuffed skin—and elbows . . . were tha like that? I were. When I was a nip fishing in grates and drains thinking it were all water so . . . did you think that? I did.

A dog bit my cheek after I furred him ever so gentle . . . a scottie and he wouldn't let go.

I'm a kriegie.

TANKY *walks round again.* DINGO *has not stopped walking.*

DINGO: It's a nickname—helps us English to reduce it to its proper size . . . minimises the position like bomb happy does—you could laugh about bomb happy and forget how they sit and shit . . .

. . . their trousers.

Shows you're not alone—coined by the officers but filtered down.

TANKY: I'm a bloody kriegie.

DINGO: In a cell.

I said at the time name, rank and number and regiment and how many rounds I had in my rifle and morale was pisspoor. And the password was TOOTING and the countersign was BEC.

TANKY: Ooh 'eck. I said it was LIVERPOOL STREET.

DINGO: No matter—bloke next door said nothing and look what happened to him . . . his trouble was he looked intelligent and a gentleman.

TANKY: They don't know much, do they?

DINGO: Didn't see how he could be only a trooper name, rank and number and the King is at Buckingham Palace.

On the ropes again—arms expansive and very free . . . their gestures give the lie to the words.

Last to have a shelter.
And always prepared to fight his own battles.
In the bag.
In the bag, Tanky. (*With great delight.*)

TANKY: In a camp.

DINGO: Round this camp have you seen? Round this camp —next time take it in—round this camp there's barbed wire.

TANKY: I've seen it.

DINGO: Doubled up.

TANKY: Waste of good wire. I see it coming in and going out.

DINGO: With machine guns winking black eyed—from those towers—swinging winking pushing a black finger between my shoulders.

TANKY: I don't like going out.

DINGO: It's all right.

TANKY: I like the woods—but I don't like going out . . .

and the dogs watching us. They ought to know we're not going to. . . .

DINGO: It's a lovely justification. I wish they had a few more guards . . . young sprightly lads who could grab my ankle should I falter.

Old Dot and Carry would have me in Brighton before he stopped coughing.

They are close together again now. A pause.

TANKY: Brighton. (*He shivers.*)

Cold now—and Worthing stinks from the fish on the beach and there's that camp I'd be in—waiting . . . waiting for the invasion.

Outside the DOG *howls again.* TANKS *clutches* DINGO.

You could never hope to get outside. Outside—there's these dogs trained to kill legs and throats—at your face. . . .

DINGO: Outside there's a war on. Inside—I'm taking up surgery.

TANKY: And I'm taking up nothing.

DINGO: You can be two's up. (*He takes a thick volume from the inside of his greatcoat.*)

TANKY: How long does it take to be a surgeon?

DINGO (*flicks through the book and looks at the last page number*): Taking everything into consideration and the fact that they've only just given the Home Guard rifles—I'm a slow reader.

TANKY: They get good money don't they?

DINGO: No—they do it for love and the hope that they might be the very first Home Guard Field-Marshal . . . L.D.V. and scar.

TANKY: I'm doing long-distance lorry driving.

They sit back to back and DINGO *reads his book.* TANKY *drives his long-distance lorry.*

DINGO: And sodall ambition.

TANKY: Heavy goods—change up.

DINGO: When you reflect on it—there are few occupations soldiering fits you to.

TANKY: Long distance lorry driving.

DINGO: That's one—and there's digging.

Who wants to be a digger all his life? Don't be a digger all your life. Take a day off to dig your own grave. (*An intense aside—vehement but soft, like the lucid phase of a fever.*)

TANKY *doesn't notice the quickening. He wipes his windscreen.*

I'll not dig my own grave . . . dig his first. I'll die screaming the more I slip—my fingers barbs—hooks . . . fish bones in the throat of death. Still when I'm cold, gob fresh shut and tied round my best shave ever, blood and spunk lead in a pencil—pennies on my eyes; still will I scream too passionful for ears of any but those that are still me.

TANKY: Long distance coaches—chara's.

DINGO: That's one—and there's ghosting.

There's always ghosting for those that soldier on and end their soldiering in the time honoured way.

Should I be a ghost—and I will be with all my tight holding on, shouldn't be a bit surprised . . . I'll make sure I do my ghosting in the sand table rooms of Sandhurst.

Do you hear?

TANKY: Change down.

DINGO: I'll be there. Whenever there's a Tactical Exercise

Without Troops—I'll stand in for the blood and snot. I'll be there—twirling in the air behind them.

Plot a move to that finger ridged hill of sand where the sponge trees shiver. One troop up one tank up one head up out of the rattling ronson—twirling on the vane sight I'll whisper "k'you darling—should have died in my wanker by rights."

TANKY: We'll do it yet Dingo.

DINGO: We'll do it yet Tanky. (*Eyes up to heaven.*)

He might—if he don't get caught, but I would not give a little boy's knot for his chances.

TANKY: We'll be there.

DINGO: Long distance lorry driving.

TANKY: Too true—heavy goods.

DINGO: There's that—and there's just two more.

Before the war—I brought up my ring to tongue my toes at the sight of sparrow raked by a cat . . . mention maternity whilst eating and I'd peck at my food.

TANKY: I'm like that.

DINGO: Still?

Stick to driving.

With me—the sights I've seen—the indifferentism—the dull in my head for red on my boots and what you might step on in the night . . . the normalcy of mates cut to chunks—stands me in good stead.

In very good stead.

I think of the two I've done right to settle for surgeon.

TANKY: You've chosen a good career there.

DINGO: Bloke at school took up butchering—took his thumb right off and he snuffed it—blood took poison.

TANKY: Ackers in that, you know.

DINGO: I think I've done the right thing to opt for surgery.
TANKY: Get the right tuition.
DINGO: It's all in here.
TANKY: If I could have got on driving.

They get up and start their perambulation. DINGO *reads his book.*

Two's up on the book then.
There's no books you can get on long distance lorry driving.

DINGO: You could get a handbook.
TANKY: I could go over the roads.
I told them I wanted driving—their remark to me in reply was they wasn't running the war for me, my lad. . . .

DINGO: Who, then?
TANKY: Not you, then?
DINGO: Not me.
TANKY: Nor me.
They told me. If they're not running it for me or thee. . . .

DINGO: Stands to reason they're not running it for them. . . .
TANKY: Who?
DINGO: You've seen them.

They stand cold still. And they listen and look at the wire—the wind flutters some striped shreds. And a DOG *howls again.*

TANKY: Why?
DINGO: I'd run a war for them—I'd run the hardest war of all for them.

Live tunneling under stage.

I might even . . . in a cell.

TANKY: What's that?

DINGO: In a cell. . . .

TANKY: Underneath.

DINGO: Don't hear it.

Nothing—don't want to hear it.

TANKY: Unless it's the dogs.

DINGO: I'm in a room.

TANKY: And me—in this room.

DINGO: In this hut.

TANKY: Hut.

DINGO: Block.

TANKY: Block.

They're getting happier as they get nearer the ropes.

DINGO: Stalag.

TANKY: Stalag.

DINGO: Enemy country.

TANKY: Enemy.

DINGO: Antagonistic populace.

TANKY: Yes.

DINGO: Who don't speak the language.

TANKY: No.

DINGO: What's more—no signposts.

TANKY: What's more—no signposts. (*Expansive arms out happiness.*)

DINGO: You could get lost out there.

TANKY: Yes.

They come together and hug each other.

DINGO: You could get very lost out there.

TANKY: You could get very lost out there.

DINGO: You know—over the years—before I qualify for

my finals as a surgeon . . . you are going to get on my wick already raw.

TANKY: I'll try not to. I'll try not to—not to. . . . (*Like a bird he begins to flutter.*)

DINGO: Bloke I know is studying engineering by the light from his little lamp.

TANKY: Those little lamps.

Live tunnelling under stage.

(*But tries to hold himself down.*) Listen.

DINGO: Escaping. (*He puts his ear down to the ground.*) In a tunnel.

TANKY: Bloody fools. (*He pushes himself against the rope.*) They'll be back—you'll be back.

DINGO: Where are you going then?

TANKY: Don't know when they're well off. (*He throws himself a bit harder at the ropes.*)

DINGO: Shall I thump the top and put the shits up them? Shall I bang so ceiling comes closer and little lamps flutter . . . so they think it's a Jerry. . . . (*He does with his fists—a frenzy of thumps and up on his feet.*)

TANKY *throws himself hard at the ropes and bounces back to sit on his arse, legs out.*

TANKY: Talking of Jerries—they've got some lovely roads for long distance.

Miles you can go.

DINGO: Those little lamps are rather intriguing—it might be worth explaining those little lamps to put you clearly in the picture.

TANKY: Here. Collection.

DINGO: Do you mind letting me tell them about the little lamps?

TANKY: No—you tell them about the little lamps we prisoners of war make . . . tell them.

DINGO: What are you holding your hat out for?

TANKY: I think they might find it rather intriguing.

DINGO: What you do—is you take some margarine.

TANKY: The Russians don't get enough to eat.

DINGO: And a klim tin.

TANKY: There's a collection for the Russians.

DINGO: Plenty of margarine.

Why didn't you tell me—you could have had my margarine. . . .

TANKY: Oh—I didn't know.

DINGO: Now I've been and rendered it down. . . .

TANKY: That's good—I'm terrified of the dark.

DINGO: For one of those little intriguing lamps.

TANKY: For when the lights go. (*He is suddenly active and throws himself at the front ropes again as the lights go off. Lands in a curled up ball—whimpering. His hands pulling his head down back into the solid of his curled tight body.*)

DINGO (*goes spare; leaps over the ropes and stamps and rails the switcher-off of the light*): That's sheer bloody-mindedness—you're being sheer bloody minded—you. . . .

TANKY: Light your little lamp.

DINGO: I can't light my little lamp.

TANKY: Light your little ingenious lamp.

DINGO: I can't light my little bloody lamp. I haven't got a little twatting lamp.

TANKY: Why?

DINGO: Because.

Searchlights flick.

See they've got light for that. Sheer hard Kraut bloodymindedness—that and the white stinking cabbage . . . and the bread and the soup—sheer bloody Bosche bloodmindedness. Fuck the common market.

TANKY: I'm dark. I'm cold. Where's your little lamp?

DINGO: Where? I gave my little lamp to the Russians.

TANKY: What you do that for?

DINGO: For them to eat.

TANKY: Sheer bloody useless—let them eat their own lamps.

He's up and straight for the ropes. But he stops and just touches them before rolling up again in a ball and whimpering.

I can't see to drive.

DINGO: Let me feel you for surgery. (*He starts to climb back in.*)

BLACKOUT

Scene Two

The beaches of Normandy. The COMIC *sits on the beaches and lets the head he has on him loll and shake and be all his parts in turn.*

COMIC: Get off my shoulders.

My head.

My head says, what does my head say, how many are dead does it say . . . what is dead to my head? What? There is no dead—there is nothing dead, I have them up and walking.

All the lovely soldier boys.

Good luck to each one of you and good hunting on the mainland of Europe.

We mothers must grin and bear it.

It is becoming increasingly difficult to grin.

Watch my other head. My other head is horrible, that's the head to watch . . . don't watch this head . . . this head will say:

As a mother who is lying ill with cancer and whose two boys are serving overseas, I feel I must write to express my deep appreciation of the splendid arrangements that were made for leave for boys from. . . .

No wonder the armies in your command are proved invincible in this war. Your men are treated like human beings. . . . Let no man surrender as long as he is wounded and can fight.

Do your sailors sing? In that case we will sing "Onward Christian Soldiers."

MOGG: Are you talking to me?

COMIC: I am talking to me.

MOGG: There is a bloke here who hits all officers.

COMIC: I'm his mother.

Can I see him?

MOGG: He's being repaired.

COMIC: My great passion in life is to see things being repaired as this is so much more interesting than seeing them whole. Totally mauled, all mauled, all totally mauled around here.

This would be a great place for my cheery old friend Sir Herbert Barker—bone setter . . . how many healthy, active people there are in Britain today who would still be cripples or in constant pain, but for Sir Herbert Barker's wonderful gift.

Now what have we here walking down yon country lane?

Baaaaaaaaaaaaaaaaaaaaaaaaa. The spectacle of wounded and terrified animals on the battlefield is in some ways the most pathetic sight of all, woof woof, down boy, are you looking for master . . . mooooooooooooooo, mooooooooooooooo, old girl, do you want a milkies? The memory of that moo haunts me still. Advance and retreat allow no time for milking. Baaaaaaaaaaaaaaaa, baaaaaaaaa, it was in a farmyard in an area Jerry was still disputing with us that I saw the little lamb . . . clear orf, matey . . . we all know that both dogs and horses hate being watched while they eat, possibly the British soldier feels the same way about it. . . .

MOGG: Sir—may I retire?

COMIC: Why?

MOGG: Sir, I have been hit three times.

COMIC: I have not touched you.

MOGG: Sir—you are sitting on me.

COMIC: How proud your mother will be to learn this.

MOGG: Sir, I would like to give you a testimonial . . . may I write you a letter?

COMIC: You may. Write it now.

MOGG: Sir,

A man of discipline and orderly mind, you nevertheless enjoy the odder, more fantastic side of war—a strict man, you are no sober sides, you have captured the imagination of the world, not only because of your ability as a soldier but because you bring to modern times the spirit of medieval wars, when fighting was romantic and glorious. . . .

COMIC: That is quite amazing because I've got a very funny face. . . .

MOGG: I am grateful to have been of your army . . . I am, sir, your obedient servant 14417695 Private Mogg. M.

I can smell them . . . there are Germans.

COMIC: Now then—that smacks of bellyaching to me, I would be the first to be informed if there were Germans about . . . you are a very fine and dutiful armchair of a private soldier and I am glad I have got you, but you are not fully in the picture, you are concerned with grains of sand, you are seeing trees where you should see woods, you would make an excellent sergeant major of Pioneers but you would never make a general . . . today we will fight the battle of Normandy and it will be terrific, terrific, I looked over the ground with a fine tooth comb before I sat down on you . . . if there are Germans within two hundred years I should be very surprised and dead as I expected you to be with all these poor boys lying around. . . .

MOGG: But I am not dead. If I point the Germans out to you, will you make me a sergeant major?

COMIC: I will, I will do more, I will let you wear my funny hat.

BLACKOUT

Scene Three

MOGG stands in the boxing ring in a searchlight beam. He is dressed as a sergeant major and a Hero and very smart. A hint of stained glass in his uniform.

TANKY is in the ring huddled up in the far corner.

DINGO is half over the ropes and half not. When MOGG appears he stays one leg over for a few speeches.

MOGG: In the field.
TANKY: Don't hit me.
DINGO: What?
MOGG: In the field—Sergeant Major in the field.
DINGO: It means nothing to me.
TANKY: Have you got a little lamp?
MOGG: I got promoted to Sergeant Major in the field.
DINGO: You can't have surgery. I bagged surgery weeks ago didn't I Tanky? There's only one book—come out from your womb Tanky and tell him—back me up.

You haven't got the intelligence anyway.

TANKY: It's cold.
MOGG: Who's senior soldier?
DINGO: Who opened the gate?

MOGG: Who's in command.

DINGO: Who let you in?

MOGG: In the field for bravery I was promoted to Sergeant Major and I would have gone on to do great things in the field.

DINGO: Looking for a field sir?

TANKY: It's cold.

DINGO: There's a wind up your back. It's come from the plains of Siberia . . .

MOGG: I've found a field.

DINGO: . . . from the parade ground Catterick. Should you be looking for a field—I know of a field. . . .

MOGG: I've found it.

DINGO: You'll be all right then sir.

Only—if it doesn't turn out right sir . . . you might like to try a wider field—turn right at the about two hundred yards till you get to the wire then trip it. . . .

MOGG: I know you.

DINGO: I know you.

TANKY: I'm starved—born in a field?

DINGO: I'm cold too.

MOGG: I should think you are.

DINGO: Well—I'll tell you. How we are with the commandant . . . that's how we are. (*Two fingers crossed under* MOGG*'s nose.*)

And that's him on top. Chuffed.

And that's us underneath—chuffed highly.

TANKY: Old Dot and Carry One.

DINGO: That's him.

TANKY: That's him—he's all right.

DINGO: On top—and that's us underneath and I'm studying surgery. . . .

TANKY: And I'm doing long-distance lorry driving.

DINGO: When I'm not working on agriculture in a supervisory capacity because I'm a lance corporal. . . .

TANKY: He supervises me.

DINGO: I put myself on orders. Next week I'm going to be a sergeant.

MOGG: I find you disgusting.

DINGO: You find us chuffed.

MOGG: I find you collaborating.

DINGO: You find us living.

TANKY: We only chop trees.

DINGO: Geneva says work—and non-commissioned officers in a supervisory capacity. That's me.

MOGG: King's Rules and Regs says escape. And harry—and tie them down to running after you—and keep the manpower tight and concentrated on watching you.

DINGO: They do. Listen.

The sound of scraping and a swish sucking noise.

Under here. Under my very feet as I talk to you now there's officers struggling like blacks and scraping away the very earth from under our very feet.

There's a dienst on.

But not us—officers only . . . like pissups all night and resigning.

It's the way they're brought up.

We can't fit it in—what with Geneva convention graft and studying for a surgeon—we don't have the energy for it.

TANKY: I've hurt my back.

DINGO: He's not well for escaping—and I get terrible claustrophobia in tunnels and wooden horses.

Don't I?

TANKY: All I want is some light.

DINGO: Can you just move over so the edge of your heroic light that you've no doubt earned in the field. . . .

MOGG: For singled handed. . . .

DINGO: Yes—can you stand so it just tips some over my mate.

MOGG: Get up . . . you disgust me.

DINGO: Get up . . . you disgust him.

TANKY *rises in the air and slides down as a hole in the ground is opened.*

A FIGURE *comes out—just head and shoulders. The* NAVIGATING OFFICER *that we last saw in the desert going over the top gloriously is now escaping gloriously. At least—his head and shoulders are.*

NAVIGATING OFFICER: I'm a British Officer.

MOGG *leaps to attention and flings him one up.*

MOGG: Sir!

NAVIGATING OFFICER: This is Coblitz.

MOGG: Sir. No, sir. If you want Coblitz—that's outside the wire in Westphalia about two or six kilometres this side of Munster. . . .

NAVIGATING OFFICER: I'm an escaping navigating officer. I know you.

DINGO: I know you.

NAVIGATING OFFICER: I know Coblitz when I see it. Cave! (*He bobs down and is gone.*)

MOGG: Did you see that!

DINGO: Very impressive.

MOGG: Did you see that—you loosebound defeatist? (*He* kicks TANKY *hard*—TANKY *curls up tighter.*)

TANKY: Oooooooooh. That hurt.

MOGG: Get to your feet—on your feet where an officer's been. You disgust me.

DINGO: You disgust him Tanky.

MOGG: And you—you make me want to throw up.

DINGO: Well—you know what I'm like—sick making.

MOGG: Up.

TANKY: You can't make me. I can't get up—it's the dark.

DINGO: It's not that dark.

TANKY: I have the horror of the dark—tell him.

MOGG (*kicks* TANKY *again*): Where's your head—let's see your head for my boot—I want to kick your head.

DINGO: He doesn't like the dark—not since he nearly died in the dark.

TANKY: I couldn't get out of this tank—oooh that hurt—you're hurting.

I have to sleep near the window. . . .

MOGG: When I've finished with you—you'll want to escape—when I've finished with you—you'll be over that wire like a lot of happy harriers—you'll beg me to shove you up a tunnel. Come out—till I stamp on your head.

TANKY: Hey . . . that hurt again.

MOGG: Do you see?

DINGO: I see.

MOGG: As an example that's all.

TANKY: Tell him to jack it in.

DINGO: He won't Tanky—he's found his field.

MOGG: The sooner you bring out your head—the sooner you'll see some light.

The light is switched on again. and TANKY *looks out. He looks at* MOGG *and curls up again. He beats the floor.*

TANKY: I thought we'd finished with that, there's always something else. . . .

MOGG: Come out.

DINGO: He doesn't like officers either—not since he nearly died from associating with an officer.

MOGG: I'm not an officer.

DINGO: Keep sweating.

MOGG: I'm proud of my rank—promoted in the field.

DINGO: In his state—you're all the same. And you're a hero—he doesn't like heroes either.

TANKY: Not since a hero nearly stuck his bayonet in my tummy. Once.

MOGG: You're a collaborating shagnasty—what are you?

TANKY: Oooooooh.

DINGO: You're going to make this Stalag the smartest Stalag in enemy occupied whatever. . . .

MOGG: Right. What are you?

TANKY: A collaborating . . . sir.

MOGG: A collaborating what?

TANKY: Yes.

MOGG: Where's your head—bring your head out till I open it. Where is it?

TANKY: Oooooh.

DINGO: You've found your field, then?
Who's on outside area?

MOGG *looks at* DINGO *and thinks—at the same time he kicks* TANKY *hard absent mindedly but hard on the end of every question regardless of whether* TANKY *answers or not.*

MOGG: The outside area is zift. What is it?

TANKY: Ooooh—zift. . . .

MOGG: Sir.

TANKY: I was going to say that, sir. Sir.

DINGO: All the stones want dressing off.

MOGG: Wants to look something like—what does it want to look like, Tanky?

TANKY: Somethink like—sir.

DINGO: Morale will soar.

MOGG: You see because morale is slack.

TANKY: Slack, sir.

MOGG: Don't anticipate the word of command—right?

TANKY: Right—oooooh.

DINGO: Sitting still in a prison camp is a legal offence in the military sense—or being in possession of the mind and purpose to sit still and go white in the head, likewise, but more difficult to prove.

And because it's an offence—it can in no way be condoned.

WILLIE *sits beside him.*

He is a big, soft, lovable guard with lots of photographs of his children and his Frau in his inside pocket.

He hunts for them now. Hands his rifle to DINGO *while he does it.*

MOGG: Morale is shot to buggery—what is it?

TANKY: Shot. It's shot.

MOGG: What?

TANKY: Shot.

MOGG: To what?

TANKY: Shot, sir—shot, sir.

MOGG: I'll say it again son so you can digest it—hear, learn and inwardly digest. Morale is shot to buggery—what is it?

TANKY: Ooooooooh Morale see—when I were a nip with nowt but a love of Jesus and I did love Him. I expected all the time for Him to look after me—when't lads used to make me roar gi'ing me Indian burns and ear rubs I used to cry to Jesus at fost—then I didn't do owt. . . .

MOGG: Stop talking in the ranks—show us your head—bring it out so I can kick it.

DINGO: Is this your frau then Willie? I bet she belts like a little rattlesnake ey? I think she's very nice—sehr gut.

TANKY: It wor only cos of my big head—and t'way I used to talk then . . . I used to talk like they talk in Derbyshire . . . that's where I come from . . . Jesus.

Dingo—dingooooooooooooooooooo. (*He jerks out straight and tries to get up*—MOGG *kicks him hard on the head and he goes down like a stone.*)

DINGO: These your chickoes then Willie? I bet you have merry adam with them—he's a real little monkey isn't he? I think they're very nice—schone.

MOGG *kicks* TANKY'S *head again and again so it gets beaten to a jelly.*

WILLIE: Feldwebel nicht?

DINGO: That's it.

WILLIE: Ja ja.

DINGO: His career was cut short in the field of battle just when he was about to make a name for himself—he's going to make this the smartest Stalag in wherever.

WILLIE: Ja ja—heir kommt. . . .

DINGO: He's persuading Tanky to escape.

COMIC: Leave the first three rows for officers and the Commandant.

They set up the booth and the lamps light. The COMIC *is accompanied by a group of giggling* GIRLS. *Three almost identical* GIRLS *in long blonde wigs and dressing gowns.*

WILLIE: Ja—gut.

DINGO: He's already persuaded me.
I intend to escape in full view.

WILLIE: For you—the war is over—nicht?

DINGO: I thought so Willie.

WILLIE: Ho ho—sehr gut.

DINGO: Tanky.

MOGG: That's better.

DINGO: Tanky's never been the same since he lost his mate.

MOGG *leans over the rope—breathing hard.*

DINGO: Breathing heavy?

MOGG: It's a bit embarrassing.

COMIC: Stand up when the commandant arrives—normal courtesy.

MOGG: I suppose it was the excitement.

DINGO: I'm escaping—I'm bribing a guard—this one here . . . he's going to swap clothes and places and he'll be a kriegie and I'll be a goon—he'll munch Red Cross all day long and study accountancy—and I'll chew sausage and belt holy seven colours out of the Russians—that right, Willie.

MOGG: I shot my lot. He was a despicable.

DINGO: You've persuaded me.

MOGG (*notices* WILLIE *for the first time; he recovers his breath and yells*): Goon in the block.

DINGO: Where?

COMIC: Goon in the block.

DINGO: Goon in the block?

WILLIE *looks embarrassed and shifts from one foot to another.*

DINGO *still holds his rifle and bayonet.*

GIRLS: Goon in the block. (*They scream and run behind the booth.*)

DINGO: Oh—you mean Willie? Yes.

TANKY *gets up on to his knees and staggers to the rope—he bounces off it.* DINGO *hands the rifle to* WILLIE.

DINGO: Goon in the block.

TANKY: When I were a nip nobbly knees I smoothed the coat of this rough haired terrier.

They all hush—the GIRLS *peep over the top of the booth and round the sides. The* COMIC *waits tense and* DINGO *crouches down.* MOGG *stands well back from* TANKY *as the lights go out and a searchlight flicks. A* DOG *howls.*

TANKY *gets to his feet in the glare of the searchlight and staggers a bit. Then rushes the rope—bounces off.*

A great Ooooooooooooh of real disappointment goes up from all assembled. He tries again. And again. And again. And again. And again—hangs over.

WILLIE *stands underneath and pushes his bayonet into* TANKY*'s stomach and* TANKY *holds it as it goes in.*

TANKY: 'kin ell.

WILLIE *pulls it out red. And* TANKY *slumps on the ropes grinning.*

Blackout.

Applause from everybody as the lights go up.

COMIC: Hard luck.

GIRLS: Hard luck.

WILLIE *has gone and* MOGG *is down outside the ring. Very chuffed.*

A blackcloth hangs in front of the boxing ring. It is a scrim. And over the top TANKY *grins in his death.*

MOGG: Good try.

It's a lie. It's not the same, it's a great disappointment to me—another bleeding disappointment. . . . I was told and expected to be horrified when I was told, I was told it was sexual, bayonets, a sexual thing . . . no such thing. Or a bad thing, spew my ring, no such thing, it's an ordinary thing—you're better off bashing your bishop. . . .

COMIC (*in his booth; introduces the camp concert*): And now a big hand for those lovely leggy ladies, the Harry Titters girls.

Five hairy British officers dressed in wigs and bikinis do a fine number about "There's something about a soldier that is fine, fine, fine." On their exit, one goes down the trap.

COMIC: Thank you. All the world loves a Sergeant Major, and here's our own lovable one . . .

MOGG (*marches to centre of stage*): Now when I first came to this camp—morale was at a very low ebb, no spirit, no get up and go. . . .

No. . . .

No. . . .

DINGO: Hello.

MOGG: Hello what?

DINGO: Hello—what do you want? (*He stands playing the*

COMIC *in reluctant heroes—unconcerned—with a cigarette.*)

MOGG: What do I want?

DINGO: Yes—what do you require—Jack? (*He plays to the audience of* COMIC *and* GIRLS—*who lap up his mock bravado. This is the true British Squaddie. A very cheeky chappie.*)

MOGG: I've had trouble with you before haven't I?

DINGO: I shouldn't be a bit surprised. (*Large wink and a larger wide swept puff on his cigarette.*)

Does haircut ring a bell?

MOGG: Haircut?

DINGO: Hair-cut.

MOGG: Haircut rings several bells.

COMIC: Get your hair cut.

DINGO: Yes—I thought it might—I'm the bloke you always check for a haircut.

MOGG: Where was it?

DINGO: El Alamein?

MOGG: Or was it Sidi Rezegh?

DINGO: It might have been—I was excused boots at Sidi Whatsit . . . or was it Wadi Whojit? (*He puts his cigarette to his mouth and his hands in his pocket.*)

MOGG: Cold?

DINGO: Not—it was hot—very hot at Sidi Whatever.

COMIC: With luck the earth was stopped and the hounds in full cry.

DINGO: Dead right. Wadi Whojit—am I right?

You was there.

MOGG: You got cold hands?

DINGO: Nobody's ever complained before.

MOGG: Pockets.

DINGO (*tries his hands flat on his cheeks*): No. No they're not cold—feel . . . they're not cold . . . I've kept them warm in my pockets. Feel.

MOGG: I don't want to feel your bloody hands trooper.

DINGO: Bloody—speak for yourself.

COMIC: Now then. (*Annoyed. Near the knuckle that.*)

MOGG: Pockets, my lad.

Are your hands so cold you've got to keep them in your pockets—there.

DINGO: Oh no—what I'm really doing is scratching my arse—sir. (*Large and engaging grin. He's lovely.*)

MOGG: I didn't ask you where your brains were. . . .

DINGO: No. And I didn't tell you.

MOGG: I'll have you.

DINGO: You couldn't have relations.

MOGG: Heels.

DINGO *clicks his heels together and stands in the classic insolent heart of gold style beloved by our* COMIC *and the* GIRLS.

MOGG *walks slowly round him.*

DINGO *does a cigarette gag with his lighted cigarette like a good old cockney comic—he puts it in his closed mouth completely as* MOGG *walks past the front of him and then takes it out as he goes behind, puffing, eyes rolling like a good old cockney comic right and left with a grin, an inane grin like a good old cockney comic—all done with the lower lip.*

The GIRLS. *Standing in front of* DINGO *at attention or near it.*

COMIC: And now on a more serious note—a song that has been on all lips, that has kept us going through many a long and lonely night when our dear ones have seemed impossibly far away.

GIRLS: We'll all pull together.

The FIRST BLONDE *stays behind when the others exit, another going down the trap. She stays looking at* DINGO.

COMIC: They tell me, Sergeant Major, they tell me morale is at a very low ebb. . . .
MOGG: That's right.
COMIC: What will you do?
MOGG: I'll kick their teeth in.
COMIC: What do I do.
There is a code you know. What do I do if a parachutist lands in my garden? I do not give him anything. I stay put and get on with my job. This is the moment to act like a soldier.
(*He stands under the towering figure of the* COMMANDANT, *who carries a sabre. The* COMIC *looks up at him and salutes.*) My word. My word. What do I do if a German officer asks the way? I remember that he is bound to be twice as windy as me because he doesn't speak the language, I stay put and I say nothing and I carry on with my job. . . .
COMMANDANT: What is your job?
COMIC: I'm a traffic policeman.

The COMMANDANT *flourishes his sabre, which inadvertently catches the* FIRST OFFICER'S *bikini.*

FIRST BLONDE: I say I'm a British Officer.
COMMANDANT: I say. . . . I am very happy to be here, to see your concert. I want you to be the first to know that I am to be transferred to the front . . . for you the war is over, for me it is just about to begin . . . I thank you and carry on. . . .
COMIC: Talking of the Commandant, did you know he

used to be in the polizei? They told him to watch all the exits . . . he did. They sacked him, they had to . . . the crook got away up his entrance . . . that's why they purged him. . . .

FIRST BLONDE: I'm an escaping British Officer, take your hand off me. (*She leans against* DINGO *in a very coquettish manner.*)

MOGG *sits biting his nails and watching.*

DINGO: Give us a kiss sir.

FIRST BLONDE: Let go of me, I'm on and I'm a British Officer.

A scene between two BRITISH OFFICERS *at a tea party. Having tea. One* BRITISH OFFICER *hates the other and tells her so. Perhaps a few lines here from Cicely and Gwendolen,* Importance, *Act 2.*

COMMANDANT: Remember to pack my field service eyeglass and my periscope attachment for the trenches.

WILLY: Ja—Herr Commandant.

The scene over, the FIRST BLONDE *goes back to stand near* DINGO *while the other one escapes through a trap held open by the* COMIC.

FIRST BLONDE: Let go of me. I'm a British Officer.

DINGO: I can see that by the feel of your chubby cheeks.

MOGG: Section four to forty.

A brace of happy BLONDES *dance across the stage in full glare of the spotlight.*

BLONDES: Section four to forty.

FIRST BLONDE: What's section four to forty?

DINGO: When I was slack and guarded nothing but sat

all day watching stores get stolen . . . I felt my heart go pounding hard at section four to forty. . . .

Not me—him.

Didn't you, Mogg.

MOGG: Offences in relationship to the enemy punishable with death—and buggery is one . . . you.

BLONDES: Ooooooh.

COMMANDANT: Remind me to have the surgeon provide me with a spare catheter, heavy duty, French wine for the passing of. . . .

WILLIE: Jawohl—Herr Commandant.

MOGG: Every person who is subject to military law . . . and who on active service commits any of the following offences; that is to say. . . .

COMIC: Death.

COMMANDANT: Death. I love your Bernard Shaw.

MOGG: Without orders from his superior officers leaves the ranks . . . in order to secure prisoners, horses, or on pretence of taking wounded men to the rear. . . .

FIRST BLONDE: No. Let go of me. I'm a. . . .

DINGO: I can tell that by the feel of your cotton wool bubs.

FIRST BLONDE: Yes.

COMIC: Now.

FIRST BLONDE: I don't want to go. I want to stay and marry him.

DINGO: I could never marry a British Officer.

COMMANDANT: Remember to pack my leather coat and my new black and my stomach powders . . . and my waterproof sheet. . . .

All are waiting for the FIRST BLONDE *to escape in the tunnel. The* COMIC *holds the trap open and grins as the* COMMANDANT *looks his way—carefully standing in front of the open trap.*

MOGG: Having been made a prisoner of war voluntarily serves with or aids the enemy. . . .

DINGO *and the* FIRST BLONDE *cling to each other.*

DINGO: I don't love you, darling.

COMIC: You, er—a funny thing . . . you can say what you like about our lovable Commandant—but he's certainly got a key position in the Wermacht.
Or. . . .

Light back to MOGG.

COMMANDANT: Sergeant—I shall want my second best leg for the trenches and the linctus—and my leather private soldiers field equipment for my men to see I live the same conditions as them—you can carry that.

WILLIE: Jawohl—Here Commandant. Achtung.

The FIRST BLONDE *has appeared on the tunnel mouth. She scrambles out into the centre of the boxing ring. The light flicks on to her. Blinds her.*

The COMMANDANT *and* WILLIE *stand up.* MOGG *babbles.* DINGO *stands watching with his hands on his hips.*

The cloth behind MOGG *is flown away.*

The light flicks and another joins it. WILLIE *holds his rifle and bayonet at the high port.*

The COMMANDANT *draws his sabre.*

For a moment the sweeping lights stop on the escaping COMIC*—his foot in the trap.*

COMIC: Er—old Kriegies never die—they simply spade away. (*He bows. And is gone with the light.*)

The focus sharpens on the FIRST BLONDE, *who holds her hands over her eyes.*

MOGG: 2. By discharging firearms, drawing swords, beating drums, making signals, using words, flags, smoke, lights, or by means whatever. . . .

*While he shouts—the searchlights flick, whistles are blown—*DOGS *yelp and the* FIRST BLONDE *starts to throw her spangled self at the ropes in a slow pattern build-up that begins to get frenzied as* MOGG'S *speech does the same.*

COMMANDANT: Death death. (*He pokes with his sabre.*)

MOGG: . . . intentionally occasions false alarms in action, on the march, or being a soldier acting as sentinel leaves his Sunray to go in search of plunder or yoni, sleeps, is pissed at his post, leaves his post without orders from his superior officer, his guard, picquet, patrol, or post without being properly relieved in the field, in action or on the march, forces a safeguard or forces or strikes a sentinel, by word of mouth or by writing, or by making gestures or by signals spreads reports calculated to cause alarm and despondency, or does misbehave or induces others to misbehave before the enemy in such a manner as to show cowardice.

The FIRST BLONDE *throws herself at the rope and back on the bayonet of* WILLIE *who has come up through the tunnel.*

She does a mincing ladylike walk to the rope alongside the dead TANKY. *And collapses arms spread on the top rope.*

The COMMANDANT *takes the blonde wig off with his sword. And he sobs. He cries.*

Quiet. No sound. Then a DOG *howls. The light flicks on to the empty booth. All gone.*

COMMANDANT: All my chicks have flown. I was so lenient with them—now I shall never get to the front—they are keeping me from my place in the battlefield.

WILLIE: Ja ja—gut Herr Commandant, gut. I am myself, very happy, I have all the fun without being shot at, it's a soldier's dream. . . .

The COMMANDANT *goes off, distraught and helped by* WILLIE. DINGO *moves to the front of the stage and starts scraping away between his feet. He has his open book in front of him.*

DINGO: Now.

MOGG: What now?

DINGO: Now he'll go down amongst the others.

A wind. The striped pieces flutter on the wire and a wail begins.

MOGG: What you on?

DINGO: Escaping now. Sir. With this piece of bent wire—an ingenious piece of bent wire, I'm scraping my way to freedom . . . digging a shaft for my own private dienst—through solid rock under my wire.

MOGG: How long's that going to take you?

DINGO: Years, George—bleeding years, how long, that's how long. . . .

MOGG: Can't have that.

DINGO: You will have that.

MOGG: I want to do my best for you.

DINGO: My duty to escape.

MOGG: That outside area is very bad, I want all those bits of paper picked up—so much paper . . . war is full of paper, have you noticed, always tossing paper around, the desert was full of paper . . . I want it all picked up and burned. . . .

DINGO: Listen.

A wailing sound grows louder and smoke starts to drift across the sky at the back.

Old Dot and Carry . . . say one thing, one thing I shall say, we kept him from the front, kept him tied down so he couldn't unleash his brilliant strokes on the unsuspecting Imperial General Staff. . . .

They are standing in the boxing ring now. MOGG *terrified.* DINGO *looks at him and goes over to hold his hand. It is here we see how grazed* MOGG *really is.*

They start the walk around the ring holding hands and MOGG *shouting without convincing* DINGO.

MOGG: I want this to be a British Camp. It shall have a guardroom.

DINGO: It shall, stand to the guard.

MOGG: Guard turn out.

DINGO: There's only me.

MOGG: And me.

They stand in the ring holding hands and listening to the wailing which gets much louder. MOGG *rolls his eyes and watches the black smoke drifting.*

Black smoke means only one thing to me, bad cooks. . . . I want this the best organised camp wherever, right? Right?

DINGO: Right.

MOGG: Remember—this is a British Camp, not a rest

home for hook-nosed miscreants—right? There's a lot we can do, build a theatre so we can have bum-titty-bum shows like the officers have . . .

DINGO: You are not having me in sequins. . . .

MOGG: And a football pitch, you never thought of a football pitch did you—it's for your morale. . . .

This go on all the time?

DINGO: What?

MOGG: Wailing, wailing . . . eh?

DINGO: That's not us.

MOGG: Who?

DINGO: That's foreign.

MOGG: I know it's foreign.

DINGO: No British Kriegie goes on like that. . . .

MOGG: Brace him up if he does.

DINGO: Morale—their morale is shot to buggery . . . otherwise they'd be having escapes and concerts and what a life . . .

MOGG: Goon in the block.

DINGO: They're not organised, see, they've got this disadvantage, they don't take the piss out of the goons, I expect they call them guards, they don't keep on his tail, watch his funny face never knowing which way to turn, where a British Officer will pop up next . . . they need you.

MOGG: I'm needed here.

I want this camp to be the smartest Stalag this side of the Rhine . . . if we get stuck in. . . .

DINGO: There's only me.

MOGG: And me. And them. (*He looks at the two figures on the ropes.*)

Wouldn't be so bad if they hung regular.

DINGO: And I'm escaping aren't I?

MOGG: What you think—those two?
DINGO: I think they shouldn't have joined.
MOGG: Dingo. Will you, will you stand up for me?
DINGO: Is it for you?
MOGG: It's for you.
DINGO: I know what's for me.
MOGG: It's for me.
DINGO: Certainly. (*He stands up.*)
MOGG: Those two. On the wire, they're a bit near aren't they . . . after all—one is a British Officer, which one is it?
DINGO: The one with the brassiere on. He's the British Officer.
MOGG: Will you straighten your back and get your heels together? For me.
DINGO: I might. I want you to be happy.
MOGG: Perhaps if we painted them white.

(*He shoots his neck out at the two on the wire and says in his first real burst of R.S.M.*) Don't you let me down and you, you with the knickers on, officer or no bleeding officer . . . you loose me down by hanging irregular and I'll write Other Ranks pisshouse on your grave. . . .

(*Now softer and like* TANKY *was in his cell—not a shout but a pleading.*) I'll have this Stalag . . . I will call this circuit, Piccadilly Circus . . . they'll mark my words—they'll be staggered, of all the strange stories to come out of the Second World War this then surely is the strangest.

DINGO: Am I to stand here all day, back straight and heels together?
MOGG: I'd like you to call me sir.
DINGO: I always do, don't I, sir?

The wailing stops. MOGG *sighs and adjusts himself in the silence.*

MOGG: That's better. Hear myself talk.

BLACKOUT

Scene Four

NB *At Bristol this scene was played by the* COMIC *as a solo ventriloquist turn: sitting behind a hessian scrim, he played alternately to the hat/cigar and the GI helmet, which were sited on either side of him, at the appropriate moments.*

The COMIC *and* CHURCHILL.

With CHALKY *sitting between them wearing a GI helmet.*

They hold umbrellas over their heads.

COMIC: Here is a pretty pickle. The Americans want the Saar, the Frankfurt area, the Ruhr, Antwerp, and the line of the Rhine.

CHURCHILL: I want a battle.

COMIC: You're a very great man, Prime Minister, but you are a bit impatient.

CHURCHILL: It's high time you had another battle.

COMIC: I've had one.

CHURCHILL: I know. I heard the bells.

COMIC: I don't drink.

CHURCHILL: I want another one.

COMIC: You shall have another one.

CHURCHILL: Now.

COMIC: No. I shan't win if I have one now.

CHURCHILL: I want a battle now. I am determined to get as much fun and personal satisfaction as I possibly can out of this war and bring my rich and rousing personality to bear upon the men and women engaged in the day-to-day jobs of battle. . . .

COMIC: You're always fast on your heels Prime Minister. There is only one standard of physical fitness, the standard of total war . . . we must all keep up, do you get up in the morning with a glad shout on your lips?

CHURCHILL: I get up in the morning with a bottle of white wine and a wing of chicken.

COMIC: You're a very great man.

The American CHALKY *speaks. He speaks in a very high voice and impossible American accent.*

CHALKY: My Generals say I'm the best General the British ever had.

COMIC (*does a take and asks*): Will you say that again General? You're a thoroughly genuine person Ike . . . you really are, will you sign my autograph book before you go?

CHURCHILL: I will.

COMIC: I've got yours Prime Minister.

CHURCHILL: I want a battle now.

COMIC: I shan't win if I have one now.

AMERICAN: I agree.

Let me go on to Falaise and we'll drive the British back into the sea for another Dunkirk.

CHURCHILL: Who said that?

COMIC: He's a very great and good man but he is an American . . . don't worry Prime Minister—we cannot come out through Dunkirk as the Germans still hold that place . . . are you full of binge? I have a master plan.

AMERICAN: Bradley has called your plan the most imaginative of the whole war . . . but he doesn't like it.

COMIC: I don't like it.

I don't like it. It's a hard nut to crack, it shall be called Market Garden and I don't like it, but I'm going to do it. . . . None of us like it.

CHURCHILL: I like it.

It will gleam and flow in the annals of history.
I want to see it.

COMIC: There's nothing to see.

CHURCHILL: There must be.

COMIC: No, really.

CHURCHILL: Don't try to tell me that. I was at Bull Run . . . I mean Omdurman. . . .

COMIC: I wasn't. I wasn't at Dieppe and I'm not going to be at Arnhem. . . .

There's really nothing to see. You are a very great man but there is nothing to see, sit down and try harder. . . .

CHURCHILL: Don't give me that. If there's nothing to see—why do you keep doing it.

COMIC: You keep telling me to.

CHURCHILL: That's right. Because I want to see. . . .

COMIC: I don't want to see.

AMERICAN: I agree.

COMIC: Good. You're a great man and a good man for an American man. . . . Will you write a letter saying you completely agree and showing your wonderful humanity in your own thoroughly personal way . . . because although I would never dream of discussing such things in a lavatory, I think my plan is full of holes. . . .

Ahhhhhhhhhhhhhh, Ahhhhhhhhhhhhhhh. Ar-rrrhem! Arnhem.

A silence as they contemplate—the COMIC *then gives an apologetic little laugh.*

Dropped a large one there, didn't we . . . have you seen me balance a fly whisk on one finger?

BLACKOUT

DOCTOR (*speaking over sounds of battle*): Where does it hurt—in the stomach—can you feel anything in your stomach son—your back, my back, your leg . . . throat, say if you feel, feel, the stump requires copious dressings and firm bandaging. Three inches above the elbow joint, wrist—conservation of the hand is of vital importance, thumbs, fingers, or parts of them must be preserved if visible, keep your head up son, blood down his throat, I told you to keep his head up, you are standing on his entrails, don't pull, for God's sake don't pull, of course he is screaming. . . .

Scene Five

The camp paraded for the entry of the Allies, headed by the COMIC.

MOGG: Stand still. (*He is very nervous of what will be thought of his camp. The two bodies are dressed off better.* MOGG, *still nervous, pulls at* TANKY *in his greatcoat. To make the greatcoat hang better.*)

DINGO *and* WILLIE *parade.*

Act casual.

Now then . . . when I give the word of command I want to see you snap into it, wait for it now . . .

DINGO *looks anxious and stamps at the ground, scratches at the ground with his boot.*

. . . don't flap, panic, and you'll be all right . . . wait for it, and I'll bring you up.

DINGO: Will I go home?

MOGG: I'll see you go home, just you make this camp . . . here in the heart of Hitler's Germany . . . a camp that refused to recognise defeat . . . more escapes than that —no goon dared put his ferret face round the abort. . . .

DINGO: . . . more in fear of marching across this Sergeant Major's parade ground . . . than their own feldwebels put the fear of Christ and the Russian front up them . . .

For my wife who cries, don't cry . . . I'm coming home. . . .

MOGG: Of all the stories to come out of the Second World War . . . I'm very worried about them two. . . .

Still, at least we look something like, stand still, Willie . . . I expect they'll make allowances. . . .

DINGO: If they're going to worry about dressing off the caput mortum they're going to have their work cut out . . . I mean to say, with some camps . . . eh, Willie?

WILLIE: We didn't know.

DINGO: I don't know.

MOGG: Stand still and all will be forgiven.

The liberating music is getting louder as they wait. Standing at attention in the almost empty camp.

DINGO: He comes to me—old Willie, and he says "teach me English for after the war, to be an accountant. . . ."

MOGG: Does he?

DINGO: So I say . . . all right, Willie. . . .

MOGG: That's it, you led him on. . . .

DINGO: That's it . . . and I get off humping, and I get left alone, and I get off grafting in the forest, picking beet, humping spuds, standing hours in the pissballing rain on appeal—I teach him to slip me fags, sausage and brot. . . .

My wife—it comes as a shock, I haven't thought of you once, I have thought of you once, twice, twice I've thought of you. . . .

The music stops. There is nobody here but the music stops. A silence. And then the NAVIGATING OFFICER *appears.*

NAVIGATING OFFICER: I'm a navigating officer. This is Coblitz.

DINGO: You wouldn't want me to think of you—in this. . . .

Yes.

This is . . . is it—it will be. (*He tosses away his surgery and stands at attention looking at* MOGG. *Bewildered.*)

MOGG: No. No. This is Stalag what? What?

DINGO: What?

MOGG: Or as we prefer to call it—Chipping Sodbury . . . you want Coblitz, sir, you don't want Coblitz, have Chipping Sodbury . . . stand by the GUARD.

NAVIGATING OFFICER: You know it's terribly buck making to see this sort of thing.

COMIC (*arrives in a British warm and a switch and without his booth; he is accompanied by an* A.D.C. *and a bunch of young officers; he carries* CHALKY; *he says to great laughs and sniggers*): My wife.

Laughs.

COMIC: My mother-in-law.

A.D.C.: Of all the strange sights to come out of the Second World War . . .

COMIC: Not to mention barrage balloons.

A.D.C.: . . . you know General, this is bloody marvellous . . . in the heart of Hitler's tottering Reich . . . like on the parade ground of Caterham. . . .

MOGG: Barton Stacey actually sir, though we did our best to get our feet up.

Get your HAIRCUT! (*Carried away by the admiration of all—he has marched forward and shouted, with looks at everyone to make sure they are looking, he has marched forward and shouted at* CHALKY: *get your hair cut.*)

The COMIC *is looking at the two bodies on the wire. He shakes his head in a moment of seriousness and all stand with heads bowed. The memorial service starts.*

NB *At Bristol we used a form of service from the 30th Corp June, 1943, Tunis, which included two hymns —"O God Our Help in Ages Past," and Kipling's "Recessional and the Solemn Remembrance of the Dead."*

While they stand, TANKY *says from his place on the wire.*

TANKY: He killed me.
DINGO: Who said that?
MOGG: Who said that?
TANKY: He did.
MOGG: Who said that—I'll have him—I'll have you. . . .
DINGO: You couldn't have black pudding. It'll have to be butchering. It will, how do you fancy being married to a butcher?
TANKY: He killed me.
DINGO: Tanky, come over here a minute, can you spare me a minute?
TANKY: He killed me.
DINGO: No.
TANKY: He bloody did.
DINGO: No. Look out there. . . .
TANKY: Ghoulish buggers. . . . (*He turns away from the audience.*)

DINGO (*laughs and tries to turn* TANKY *round*): Hey, hey—come on, Tanky, you're a hero, having died. . . .

TANKY: I don't hold with bleeding heroes.

DINGO: No, no, look out there, I've told you before . . . out there, mothers.

You allus appeal to the mums.

TANKY: They should be home burning their kids' toys.

DINGO: No, no—look at them, we're all going home . . . and you'll be left as a cross, so have a good look . . . now then, how did he do more than his duty, eh?

Willie?

TANKY: Not Willie, he's all right, is Willie . . . Mogg.

DINGO: No, look—see here, Tanky, if it was killing, murder, if an officer or NCO does murder when he suggests they do things, when he enthuses them with the wish to please him, for the good reasons he always has . . . if that, then, would any magistrate in the land take any notice whatsoever of a gallant war record? Eh? What do you hear them all say—eh?—Because of your gallant war record . . . because of your fine military background, eh? Now they wouldn't say that if it was murder, would they?

TANKY: He killed me.

DINGO: Look, if he killed you, if every bloke as went for a shit with a rug round him blames it on the blokes that sent him out—see my reasoning?

TANKY: He did.

DINGO: That would make all these public figures who directed the course of events, well, I hesitate to say it—every general, colonel, corporal will tell you how they hated doing it. . . .

TANKY: Shouldn't have joined, then. They all lapped it up . . . it's very interesting . . . he killed me.

And they saw it.

DINGO: I can't convince him.
FIRST BLONDE: I'm a British Officer.

The last hymn is sung of the memorial service.

A long hymn and sung in full.

The COMIC *stands in the ring with the figures of* TANKY *and the* FIRST BLONDE *hanging from the wire.*

At the end of the service there is a long silence. And then the COMIC *puts his hand out and picks up the* FIRST BLONDE*'s head. As he does so—a great wailing goes up. The wailing stops.*

MOGG: It's all right sir, it's not him.
I was going to have him painted up.
COMIC: Yes. (*He picks up the* BLONDE*'s head again.*)
FIRST BLONDE: I'm a British Officer.

MOGG *has fussed forward to deal astonishment.*

There is laughter from all assembled. The COMIC *lifts* TANKY*'s head.*

TANKY: He killed me.

At which everybody falls about again.

MOGG: Very good . . . very good.
FIRST BLONDE: I'm a British Officer in disguise.
COMIC: You're what?
Ladies and gentlemen and here is a British Officer . . . and how old are you?
FIRST BLONDE: Nineteen actually.
COMIC: Nineteen!

And a big hand for the British Officer of nineteen.

Tell me-er-lieutenant?

FIRST BLONDE: Harold.
COMIC: Harold—tell me—where were you captured?
FIRST BLONDE: I was put in the bag at Dieppe.
COMIC: Dieppe!

And a big hand for the British Officer of nineteen captured at Dieppe.

Tell me, Harold—before you were captured you gave a good account of yourself?

FIRST BLONDE: My men and I . . . we fought to the last man—I got twenty-five of them . . . it was a real killing match because we were determined to put up a really good show . . . I got some twenty-five I'm sure of and perhaps one or two more in the dark. . . .
COMIC: Twenty-five!

A very big hand for the British Officer of nineteen captured at Dieppe who got twenty-five of them.

He admits to . . . (*A wink and laughter.*)

Tell me, Harold—you got put in the bag at Dieppe—but you didn't stay there long, did you . . . they couldn't hold you in any prison camp. . . .

FIRST BLONDE: Well—I was itching to get back into the scrap.
COMIC: Scrap.
FIRST BLONDE: Before the other chaps pegged more than me.
COMIC: Lucky bastards.
FIRST BLONDE: Galling—not to be in at the death.
COMIC: Death.
FIRST BLONDE: So I got first reserve on a dienst and hard cheese; the other chap caught a cold . . . and was in tears when I had to field in his place.
COMIC: Hard luck.

DINGO: 'k his luck.

FIRST BLONDE: Concert party actually—we were the Harry Titters Girls . . . we had a go.

COMIC: No prison camp could hold you.

FIRST BLONDE: That was the idea.

COMIC: Away—what was your route?

FIRST BLONDE: Well—I got skewered on the wire, actually. It hurt . . . it hurt . . . it hurt.

DINGO: Right up his gonga.

MOGG: We can do without that.

DINGO: Give him a big hand.

They do.

Right round his earhole.

COMIC: And only nineteen . . . and he came all this way to be with us today . . . isn't that just superb?

Now, Harold . . . because you're nineteen and because you're dead, and because you were gallant at Dieppe . . . I'll tell you what we'll do . . . you Harold can choose any major prize you wish without answering any question at all.

Applause all round.

What's it going to be. . . . ? (*He turns the* FIRST BLONDE*'s face so that it whispers in the* COMIC*'s ear.*) What?

No-er no Harold . . . you can't have that—only the King himself can grant you that.

Yes?

No-er no Harold . . . you cannot have the Victoria Cross . . . you have chosen the one decoration it is not in my power to award.

You know the rules of the show.

Yes.

Yes Harold—I can give you the Distinguished Service Order . . . and here it is! (*To wild applause from all except* DINGO . . . *drops the* FIRST BLONDE'*s head and takes out a box containing a DSO. A special lining of purple satin and a gold clasp!*

He looks for somewhere to pin it and turns to the A.D.C., *who is clapping like a Trojan.*) They usually have a little loop don't they—don't they?

And here follows one of those delightful little official balls-ups—that is so funny.

Finally he pins it to the seat of the FIRST BLONDE'*s panties. And pats it.*

COMIC: You've got a nasty place there.
TANKY: He killed me.

More wailing and the COMIC *is beginning to be irritated.*

COMIC (*shouts*): We've all been through it you know . . . come into the pawnshop Sheila, I want to get you alone. . . .

The wailing again.

The NAVIGATING OFFICER *strides out to see what is, just what is causing the bellyaching.*

If I was a cannibal and she was breakfast, I'd have breakfast in bed . . . you know what a pity it would be to overshadow all our really practical worries with a lot of appeals about Utopias and a lot of windy academic discussions . . . have you all got Army Election Form B 2626 . . . they're all the same . . . so don't bother to look over each other's shoulder.

We have won the German war, let us now win the peace.

The COMMANDANT *waits on the fringe. He hovers nervously and takes out a cigarette. The* COMIC *fixes him with a glare and he puts the cigarette away.*

I said to them, Union Jacks flying, they came to me, and I made them wait . . . and then I said to them, I didn't talk to them . . . I said to them through an interpreter, I said who are these men, who do they want?

The COMMANDANT *holds a small white flag. He gives it a little shake.*

CHURCHILL: No Socialist system can be established . . . without some form of political police. . . .

COMIC: You're a very great man but you're going to lose the election, you are . . . you really are.

COMMANDANT: Might I say . . . the Socialists . . .

COMIC: No you may not say, who are these men . . . ?

COMMANDANT: . . . must be beaten.

COMIC: Yes you may say.

COMMANDANT: It must not happen. It would mean the ruin of Europe if the Socialists came to power in England. I have shares in the Ruhr and I hear that one of the plans is for the nationalisation of mines, this is entirely against human nature.

Now is the time to work, everybody must work, managers and men, below ground and above. . . .

What a pity it would be if we clouded these practical worries with windy theories of the individual and the State and so on.

COMIC: A mother says . . . "my son was twenty-two when

he gave his life for freedom. I am going to vote for him. He gave all he had. Perhaps he is merely a number to these so-called Britons who consider money the most important thing on earth.

"I believe Christianity is based on sharing and doing all possible for the benefit of human beings, so here is one vote on behalf of one of the Desert Rats."

The voice of her dead boy will be heard. . . .

COMMANDANT: Russian Barbarism . . .

COMIC: They came to me and they surrendered—I said . . . "who are these men."

Of the men who came to me, one took poison, one shot himself and one motor accidented himself.

The NAVIGATING OFFICER *is back—he sits on the ground and he retches.*

The others have gone to look at the wailing, which continues through until the rest of the play is ended.

COMIC (*puts his hand on* DINGO's *head and says*): Well done, thou good and faithful servant.

MOGG *pushes himself under the other hand. A* YOUNG OFFICER *stands up at the back and starts to sing "Jerusalem."*

MOGG: They're a lot of swindlers out for themselves, Conservative or Labour, it's me first all the time.

What is the use of voting. It will not make any difference.

Vote, sir—what is the good of a vote . . . all I want to vote for is my ticket, it is none of it sexy, they get you fighting by telling you it is sexy and then they let you down.

COMIC: . . . he has told me he wants a good house with a

bit of garden, he wants a job at a fair wage, no matter how hard the work may be, he wants a good home for his children and educating for them.

He wants to feel they won't have to go through what he has gone through in this war. . . .

DINGO: I want to go home. I'm shivering.

NAVIGATING OFFICER: They'll have to shoot them. They were a great mound—a wailing mound, black holes all wailing and they moved!

I'm a navigating officer, and I'm lost.

COMIC: Personal problems are taking a back seat for a moment while YOU concentrate on electing YOUR government . . . for five long years the lusty youth of this great land has bled and died. . . .

DINGO: I want to go home to my wife who cries, she has cried since the day I went away, she cried because I went away—she cried all the time I was in the drill hall down the road, she cried when I moved to Wembley Stadium, a fourpenny bus ride, she cried all week-end I was home, she has cried since 1939 . . . she doesn't cry because I'm suffering, because I'm not, she doesn't because I'm shot at . . . she cried because I've gone away, and she won't stop crying and if I go home and look at her she will stop crying and she will go out of her mind and be put in a hospital for ever, which she did, which is where she is today in 1967.

The thing I blame the bastards for more than anything is they have taken away my sorrow, like the lads, the first time I knew it was gone, like we tossed the Eyetie prisoners over the ledge to their death. British soldiers did this at Keren, we did . . . I did, over.

That's what I blame the bastards for more than

anything, chopping off, more like wearing away, rubbing down my compassion to not a thing. . . .

"Jerusalem" ends. Wailing gets louder.

What is this wailing, it was the wailing of my wife, it was the wailing of myself, it was the wailing of all that I have seen die and it was nothing . . . it is such a pity this war was not fought for them . . . I might have kept my compassion, I might have not felt guilty which I don't, because everybody will say it was fought for them.

It was not. It was fought for all the usual reasons.

DINGO *and* MOGG *move to the proscenium arch, one on each side.*

CHURCHILL: How far is the West Wall?

COMIC: Do you wish to go to the Men's Room Prime Minister?

CHURCHILL: I will wait. Is this the West Wall?

COMIC: It is. There are a lot of photographers about.

CHURCHILL: Yes. Are they all here, all, are all my generals here?

COMIC: I'm here—your Captain.

CHURCHILL: Gentlemen, I would like to ask you all to join me in this task. Let us all urinate on the West Wall of Hitler's Germany.

This is one of those operations connected with this great war which must not be reproduced graphically. . . .

A laugh all round and a blackout.

DINGO: From where I sat I could see a childish grin of satisfaction—intense satisfaction spread all over the

Prime Minister's face as he looked down at the critical moment. . . .

COMIC: Your freedom is in danger. Will you vote?

DINGO: Too true I shall vote. I do not . . . I have not come all this way to be pissed on twice by Mr. Churchill.

TANKY: He killed me. He killed me. He killed me.

The wailing gets unbearably loud.

CURTAIN